The
Philosophical
Biographer

The
Philosophical
Biographer

Doubt and Dialectic in Johnson's

Lives of the Poets

MARTIN MANER

The University of Georgia Press

Athens and London

© 1988 by the University of Georgia Press
Athens, Georgia 30602
All rights reserved
Designed by Barbara Werden
Set in Linotron Janson
The paper in this book meets the guidelines for
permanence and durability of the Committee on
Production Guidelines for Book Longevity of the
Council on Library Resources.

Printed in the United States of America
92 91 90 89 88   5 4 3 2 1

Library of Congress Cataloging in Publication Data

Maner, Martin
The philosophical biographer

Bibliography: p.
Includes index.
1. Johnson, Samuel, 1709–1784. Lives of the poets.
2. Biography (as a literary form). 3. Johnson, Samuel,
1709–1784—Philosophy. 4. Poets, English—Biography—
History and criticism. 5. Philosophy in literature.
I. Title.
PR3537.B54M36 1988   821'.009 [B]   87-34296
ISBN 0-8203-1038-7 (alk. paper)

British Library Cataloging in Publication Data available

Chapter 3 appeared as "Samuel Johnson, Scepticism, and Biography" in
Biography: An Interdisciplinary Quarterly, © 1987 by the Biographical
Research Center.

Contents

Acknowledgments

I owe a permanent debt of gratitude to the late Irvin Ehrenpreis, who set an inspiring example through his teaching, his scholarship, and his admiration for Samuel Johnson.

I also thank my colleagues in the Wright State English Department for their encouragement—especially Larry Hussman, Peter Bracher, and Gary Pacernick for constant moral support and Tom Whissen for helping to keep me aware that good expository prose should be straightforward and unpretentious.

I appreciate the help I received from the resources and personnel of the Folger, Cornell, University of Virginia, Ohio State, University of Dayton, Youngstown State, Wittenberg, and Wright State University libraries.

Earlier versions of chapters 2, 3, 4, 5, and 6 appeared as articles in, respectively, *American Imago*, *Biography*, *Genre*, *Age of Johnson*, and *Philological Quarterly*. I thank the publishers for permission to reprint these.

I also wish to thank the College of Liberal Arts of Wright State University, under the direction of Dean Perry Moore, for giving me financial help and time to work. The college has given me two research grants and leaves of absence, and its supportive environment has enabled me to pursue interests as diverse as jazz and Johnson.

Thanks above all to Elizabeth, Jaimie, and Karen, who have brought new joy and meaning to my life.

The
Philosophical
Biographer

One

Introduction

Why write a book about doubt and dialectic in Johnson's *Lives*? From a specialist's viewpoint, the topic may look shopworn; scarcely a single Johnsonian of recent years has failed to mention Johnson's dialectical tendencies, and the leading Johnsonians, notably W. J. Bate and Donald Greene, have devoted much attention to Johnson's skeptical and "bisociative" habits of mind, while Johnson's skeptical approach to biography has been discussed by Robert Folkenflik, the most recent analyst of the *Lives (Samuel Johnson, Biographer* 216–18).

I believe that Johnson's bisociative tendencies merit another look, especially in light of a well-established trend in studies of Johnson and other eighteenth-century British writers. I refer to the continuing development of a significant body of scholarly work dealing with the interrelations between epistemology and literature in the seventeenth and eighteenth centuries. In this study I attempt to link Johnson's dialectic with the epistemological presuppositions that support it.

Critics have long been concerned with the influence of Locke on Johnson and his contemporaries, but during roughly the past fifteen years we have seen an increasing concentration on the broader subject of epistemological influences upon literature in Johnson's century and in the preceding one. To attempt a summary or synthesis at this point would be futile and distracting, but a glance at my bibliography will show that a survey of writers who have dealt directly or in passing with such issues would have to include Uphaus, Rothstein, Patey, Trowbridge, Shapiro, Braudy, Chapin, Edinger, Dussinger, Kahn, Noxon, Tarbet, Tavor, Kenshur, and Walker.

A curious thing about this concentration of interest has been its tendency to focus on narrative fiction. One might suspect that theories of knowledge and inquiry would show their influence most clearly in a nonfictional form such as biography, a genre fraught with epistemological problems and uncertainties; recent criticism, however, has more often focused on the novel, finding in it "a concern with epistemological inquiry" that gave rise to generic conventions typical of the period (Rothstein 3). An epistemological concern with analogies and discriminations was especially typical of "a branch of literature so empirical in texture as fiction," Rothstein suggests (16), alluding to the verisimilitude, or truth to experience, required of the novelist, but perhaps no genre is as "empirical in texture" as biography.

It is possible, in fact, that a shift of epistemological paradigm may have been one cause of the rise of biography as a genre. It is worth noting that Ian Watt's attempt in *The Rise of the Novel* to relate the rise of realistic fiction to new philosophical trends scarcely mentioned biography despite the fact that biography's need to evolve techniques of "formal realism" was just as pressing as the novel's. Perhaps biography, even more clearly than fiction, can be shown to carry the marks of epistemological influence.

Initially my interest in Johnson's *Lives* was aroused by what seemed to be rhetorical strategies of restraint in Johnson's *Life of Savage*. Repeatedly in that biography Johnson seems to retreat from one sort of emotional response and to invoke another, countervailing one; he seems to oscillate between comic and pathetic modes especially. The critics who attributed this apparent ambivalence to the complexities of Johnson's personal relationship with Savage, it seemed to me, were overlooking the way Johnson employs such oscillations—throughout his writings but especially in the *Lives*—in the interest of attaining a certain type of knowledge. These characteristic reversals of tone and attitude can be seen as manifestations, sometimes planned and sometimes spontaneous, of something deeper: a method of thinking about human experience that begins with, and constantly returns to, doubt—about how to feel, about how to interpret, and about how to value.

As I studied Johnson's relationship to the philosophical skepticism of his century and the preceding ones, looking for direct philosophical influences upon his biographical practice, I found not one but a set of influences, less direct but more pervasive than I had supposed. Johnson's biographical doubts, whatever the seeming narrowness of my topic, do illustrate a wide range of tendencies in eighteenth-century literature.

In particular, I am concerned with a cluster of habitual patterns of thought characteristic of Johnson and his era, especially the habit of constantly drawing attention to the difference between appearances and realities. As a basis for argument, this form of doubt carried associations with Pyrrhonist skepticism, but it became an important issue for empiricism through the questions it raised about scientific knowledge in general. Newton's experiments with prisms, for example, dramatized the physical basis of such a distinction between appearance and reality in a way the layman could readily grasp: when we split light into its spectral components, we see that white light is demonstrably a mixture of constituent parts which our perceptual apparatus "fuses" for us. Our knowledge is shown to be based on misleading data, even (or especially) in the realm of vision, the king of the senses, which is identified with credibility itself. (Seeing is believing.) In its ability to penetrate analytically into the hidden structure of things, empirical science reinforced the skeptical case for epistemological indeterminacy based on sensory indeterminacy.

One result of this doubt about the evidence of our senses, to put it simply, was that an entire period became obsessed with seeing clearly. The ancient Greek skeptic could cite the apparent bending of an object seen half in, half out of water, as evidence for sensory indeterminacy, but that sort of sensory distortion is too obviously a special case, a sort of trick water plays upon us, that we learn to compensate for. Newton's experiment, however, demonstrates that vision itself is "flawed" in that it is capable of discerning not the component primary qualities but only those mixtures that strike the sensorium as "fused" secondary qualities.

Thus skepticism made one especially vital contribution to the development of the epistemology of science: those skeptical tropes which emphasized the problematic, uncertain, and sometimes deceptive relationship between sense perceptions and our ideas about things helped to force a new and acute consciousness of such distinctions as Locke drew between primary and secondary qualities and between real and nominal essences. As A. D. Nuttall puts it,

> Locke means several things at once by this doctrine [of real and nominal essences]. First is the notion that the properties we can talk about are really the product of an inner material constitution itself inaccessible to observation. I can *say* that I know that the ring on my finger is gold because of its "colour, weight, fusibility, fixedness, &c." if I wish. But all these qualities depend on "the real constitution of its insensible parts," and this we cannot perceive. [17–18]

So pervasive has this distinction become, and so thoroughly ac-
customed are we to a scientific episteme that associates "real"
knowledge with the knowledge of hidden inner structure ana-
lyzed in "mathematically measurable qualities" as opposed to
"merely sensed qualities" (Nuttall 22), that we are all too liable to
forget what Nuttall calls "the grand paradox of English empiricism": "its hostility to experience" (23).

In literary criticism of Johnson this forgetting has led to a subtle misrepresentation of his empiricism. In dismantling the old
imago, Johnson the dogmatic generalizer, and erecting a new one,
Johnson the empiricist, contemporary critics have rightly stressed
Johnson's openness to experience and the perpetual grounding of
his responses in the direct perception of life, but they have forgotten that empiricism also entails a hostility to experience. If one
wishes to reach empirically the formula for an "ideal" trajectory,
one must strip away the influence of air resistance in order to see
that the underlying form is parabolic, just as Galileo had to disregard or compensate for the influence of friction in arriving at
the formulas which correctly describe the acceleration of moving
bodies. The empirical method, as such simple instances show,
must proceed by stripping away the complexities of experience in
order to arrive at an analytic truth: "The ordinary man's uncon-
trolled experience is, from the scientist's point of view, an *embar-
ras de richesse*. . . . The scientist's first enemy is the fecundity of
experience, and his first task is to sterilize it" (Nuttall 21).

But of course the literary critics praise Johnson for generally
taking into account precisely this "fecundity of experience" in
what they call his "empiricism," by which they mean simply
"awareness of experience." Aside from this misuse of terminology
and its resulting oversimplifications, I have no quarrel with the
general reevaluation of Johnson entailed by the recent decades-
long emphasis upon his rich awareness of the emotional, the particular, the sensory, the untheoretical—all of which are aspects of

"experience" in the broad sense. However, I think a useful corrective to oversimplification might be to focus on this other side of Johnson's "empiricism": its *distrust* of experience, its skepticism, its doubts.

A characteristic Johnsonian gesture is described by the slang term "double-take," which denotes a second look occasioned by doubt of the evidence of one's senses, and as the very phrasing of my preceding sentence suggests, it is only a short distance from doubting what we call the *evidence* of one's senses to a habit of thinking in terms of evidence generally, and to a habit of thinking that consistently "takes" testimony "double," as though experience came to us in the form of testimony delivered by adversaries before a judgment bench. In this context it is interesting that the very concept of "reasonable doubt" in trial by jury is coeval in development with the probabilism whose influence in literature critics are now examining.[1]

Doubt and dialectic work together to constitute a way of knowing. Dialectic, in the sense of a pattern of thought based upon contrasting or antithetical terms, constantly couches problems of judgment in terms of opposed probabilities which the mind must weigh and evaluate. Whereas the skeptic employs such oppositions in order to cultivate aporia, or suspension of judgment, Johnson uses them to cultivate the engagement of a constantly active process of judgment.

My whole argument is built around a set of interrelated terms: doubt, dialectic, skepticism, judgment, and probability. These are all crucial items of diction for anyone who would describe the shift of epistemological paradigm that occurred during Johnson's and the preceding century. Gradually a concept of human knowledge centered upon the concept of deductive certainty gave way to one centered upon the concept of inductive probability. The change was associated with a complex set of historical and intellectual forces: antischolasticism, the revival of skepticism, the rise of the new science, the Augustan drive for consensus, and the rise of Lockean empiricism. I have singled out for consideration a few influences among many.

The rise in the importance of biography in the eighteenth century is associated more with Johnson's influence and example than with anyone else's, and one relatively unexplored reason for Johnson's intense involvement with the genre may have been precisely its connection with the new paradigm of knowledge. Seen from the classical, Aristotelian perspective, biography inhabits a position low in the hierarchy of human knowledge. It deals with the particular, the historical, and the probable, so it can never be truly philosophical; it functions in the realm of opinion rather than the realm of certainty. It is a subspecies of history, which is less philosophical than poetry in any view of knowledge that sees deductive certainty as the model of knowing.

However, when seen from an empirical perspective, biography takes on new importance and dignity. If induction from experience is the basis for evaluating probability, and if probable knowledge is the basis for most of human conduct, then a literary form based upon induction from particulars may be the most philosophical of literary forms rather than the least. Perhaps the biographer who refers constantly to the probable bases for his conclusions is performing as philosophical an examination of human life as is humanly possible.

Yet it would be inaccurate to describe Johnson and his biographies as wholly representative of the new empiricism. Johnson was a transitional figure, and biography was a transitional form. On one hand, biography has traditional and classical affinities: it is more obviously and directly mimetic than many other literary forms; it has roots in ancient precedents; it draws upon the traditional rhetoric of praise and dispraise; and in Johnson's theory at least, it constantly subordinates the particular to the general, using detail and anecdote to illuminate character. On the other hand, biography has affinities that link it with the modern sensibility: precisely because it lays claim to objectivity, it raises the problem of subjectivity; its precedents include skeptical, critical biography in the pattern supplied by Bayle; the complexities of understanding a human subject force it beyond the basic polarities of praise and dispraise; and the assignment of an expressive function to details, facts, and anecdotes only raises the problem of a "forcing," rather than a discovery, of significance.

Another way of understanding Johnson's transitional position is to place him in the context of a transitional moment in the development of logic and rhetoric. In the preface that he contributed to Robert Dodsley's *The Preceptor* in 1748, Johnson suggested studying both the older, Aristotelian logic and the modern, post-Lockean logic. He wrote that the reader wanting an introduction to logic could benefit not only from such Lockean sources as William Duncan's *Elements of Logick*, a treatise contained in Dodsley's volume which applied Locke to the teaching of logic, but also from the study of Crousaz, Watts, Le Clerc, Wolff, and Locke himself. On the other hand, he subsequently suggested that traditional Peripatetic logic could be studied in the works of Sanderson, Wallis, Crackanthorp, and Aristotle (Dodsley 1:xxv–xxvi).

Johnson's *Dictionary* shows close acquaintance not just with Locke but with such adaptors of Lockean empiricism as Watts, who is cited frequently. Johnson's respect for Watts is shown by the fact that Watts was included in the *Lives* specifically at his request, and in the *Life of Watts* he respectfully singles out Watts's *Logick* as so firmly established that it "wants no private recommendation."[2] He also mentions Watts's *Improvement of the Mind* as an adaptation of Locke that is "in the highest degree useful and pleasing" (3:309). (Watts also owed much to *The Port-Royal Logic* in his stress upon the role of logic in inquiry and communication, in his ordering of the main divisions of logic, and in his treatment of various subsidiary matters [see Howell, *Eighteenth Century* 343–44].)

Johnson may also have been influenced by Duncan, whose originality lay in his treatment of inductive method in his section on judgment, which he saw as founded on intuition, experience, or testimony. In Duncan's view, intuition is the basis for scientific knowledge, but experience is the basis of natural knowledge. And since individual experience is limited, we rely also on testimony, especially with regard to the past. In evaluating historical testimony, Duncan says, we use criticism and conjecture, instruments that correspond to the demonstrative syllogisms used by science and the induction and analogy used by natural philosophy. In Duncan's emphasis upon the possibility of probable conclusions in natural philosophy and historical studies, we see "not only a renunciation of the rigidities of the old habit of mind but also a positive step forward in the development of eighteenth-century British logic" (Howell, *Eighteenth Century* 355).

In a famous aside in his *Life of Milton*, Johnson wrote: "We are perpetually moralists, but we are geometricians only by chance" (1:100). His comment arose in the context of his evaluation of the sort of educational reform that he (erroneously) claimed Milton was urging—what we might call the replacement of humanistic studies by scientific ones. But behind the antithesis which contrasts morality with geometry and which prefers frequent usefulness rather than occasional usefulness, there lies a secondary antithesis: probability and certainty. Geometry is the very model of rational certainty; applied morality is the model of probability.

It should be understood that for Johnson there are moral certainties; these are grounded upon our knowledge of God's will.

The Philosophical
Biographer

But ultimately even this knowledge rests upon testimony, a form of probable evidence; and in any case, the application of morality (that is, the application of general principles to specific cases) always carries us back to the realm of the probable. In this sense, biography is a form well adapted, perhaps *the* form best adapted, to the training of moral judgment.

Judgment is a broad and ambiguous concept in the eighteenth century, and Johnson's uses of the term, as Jean Hagstrum has shown, suggest that for him the term describes a far more creative and active faculty than any "neo-classic and Lockean conception of the cold, restraining judgment"; in Johnson's way of thinking, "the purely intellectual faculty is impelled by heat and power of its own generation" ("Johnson's Rationalism" 202). But central to Johnson's uses of the term is an epistemological concept and a rather technical one at that: judgment is that portion of the rational faculty which operates in the realm of probability and which enables us to draw probable conclusions in the absence of demonstrative certainty. As intuition is to certainty, so judgment is to probability. Intuition and judgment are two aspects of the mind's ability to perceive congruity between ideas, but judgment functions in the realm of nondemonstrable truth. For this use of the term, which emphasizes an aspect of judgment different from the concept of discrimination by which judgment was contrasted with the combinative power of wit and imagination, I take as primary warrant the careful definition Johnson offers in his *Dictionary*, where he illustrates "judgment" by quoting Shakespeare, Watts, and, most important, Locke: "The faculty, which God has given man to supply the want of certain knowledge, is *judgment*, whereby the mind takes any proposition to be true or false, without perceiving a demonstrative evidence in the proofs. *Locke.*"

In its most frequent form, judgment for Johnson entails the weighing of the relative likelihood of two juxtaposed possibilities.

Bisociative thinking, then, is part and parcel of his probabilism, because he thinks usually in terms of choice; he aims to educate the reader's judgment by constantly bringing to the surface various reasons for doubting whether one should choose A or B, and then he enacts the process of doubting, judging, and deciding.

In conceiving of judgment in this way, Johnson was influenced by a shift in concepts of probability. While the emergence of the mathematical and aleatory concept of probability was sudden and drastic, a more gradual shift occurred in the broader concept of epistemological probability: the ancient division between knowledge and opinion was being replaced by a concept of various degrees of certainty (see Hacking 12 and Barbara Shapiro 15–73).

Douglas Patey is right to emphasize that there was no sudden emergence of a literary concept of probability. For one thing, a complicating factor prevents our imagining that there was a sudden change from rationalist to empirical paradigm: the reform of logic and rhetoric, based on the idea that discourse is a single art. Knowledge and opinion might be distinct realms, Ramists could argue, but the tools of discourse used in each realm are the same.

For another thing, as Patey has shown, ancient canons for the evaluation of testimony were one early source of a preliminary concept of probability, in which the probable is simply equivalent to the generally accepted. In fact, in Patey's view, Locke's treatment of degrees of probability "amounts to little more than a repetition of older canons for judging the reliability of witnesses"; thus "Locke's distinctive contribution is his attempt to show that probable and certain knowledge arise from the same kinds of mental operation, and hence are epistemologically continuous; they differ in degree rather than in kind" (Patey 7, 27).

The Port-Royal Logic has been seen as the first modern treatment of probability, but Patey argues that it should be seen instead as a consolidation of earlier developments, its primary purpose being to instruct the layman in how to convert " 'speculative' conscience, or theoretical knowledge of the moral law, into a 'practical' conscience, a moral judgment that fits the circumstances of the given case" (57). One can argue, then, that developments in the art of moral casuistry influenced epistemology, which in turn influenced literary theory and its concept of the probable: "Until well into the eighteenth century, it was through probable signs that reasoning from effect to cause, from the 'manifest' (outer) properties of objects to their 'occult' or 'hidden' (inner) properties was understood" (35). This form of reasoning originated in ancient medical theory, which related signs or symptoms to underlying causes; from medical theory it was extrapolated to rhetoric, to casuistry, and then to literary criticism, where it became, Patey argues, the Augustan theory of literature: "The literary work is a structure of signs organized in such a way as to lead the mind to their causes" (88). Generalizations about the usual relationship between signs and underlying causes are what the period called decorums.

Patey sees a transition in the eighteenth century between hierarchical structures of signs, and horizontal ones; that is, "plot yields the stage to character; and probable signs and circumstances come gradually to lose their central place in literary theory" (89–90). I see a different sort of transition exemplified in Johnson's approach to probability in biography. In his thematic ordering of the *Lives* there is a survival of the hierarchical theory of probable signs, in that he sees persistent ironic patterns in human life that suggest typical lines of signification, as though God were instructing us through the pattern of human events. Furthermore, the biographies are constructed as paradigmatic exercises in critical and historical judgment, with Johnson firmly in control of, and carefully exemplifying, ways of reaching accurate judgment about the significance and value of human lives even while making it clear that these are probable judgments rather than final or demonstrative ones. One part of Johnson's procedure points back to a concept of universal rational significance in which God has structured the universe as a pattern of intelligible signs; another part points forward to a concept of local empirical significance in which the relationship between sign and things signified is always problematic and uncertain.

Robert Voitle has most accurately described Johnson's ambivalent position: "He retains enough of the traditional humanist attitude toward the moral function of reason so that it is fair to call him a rationalist in morals, but his epistemology is empirical" (12). Voitle carefully avoids the either/or approach to logic and epistemology, recognizing that Johnson operates both deductively and inductively, empirically and rationalistically. In granting reason a crucial role in governing moral conduct, Johnson allies himself with the rationalism of the tradition stemming from Aristotle, while in seeing reason as a faculty grounded in sense data and experience, he allies himself with the tradition stemming from Locke.

Johnsonian biography thus provides an opportunity to see some emergent and ambivalent manifestations of probabilistic modes of thought. Today's criticism has gone far toward showing how such eighteenth-century fictional conventions as journeys, inset stories, and parallel episodes function as ways of dramatizing the process of probable judgment. The purpose of such dramatization, Patey argues, is *a rectification of expectations* (214; his italics)—a way of teaching the reader to increase his enjoyment by modifying his unrealistic expectations. Later in the century, Patey suggests, judgment as the key faculty to be educated is replaced by "quasi-intuitive communion with the thoughts and feelings of others" (222).

A similar point of view is expressed by Eric Rothstein, who argues that "the most important formal procedures in the novels [of the eighteenth century] are modification and analogy" as they give rise to comparative and analogical structures; the reason is that "scientific probabilism made analogy the key to inferential knowledge" (11, 14). The fiction of this period thus provided paradigmatic exercises in probable judgment: "The ideal of discriminated variety, to which eighteenth-century readers were peculiarly alert, shows how analogy calls on the combined faculties of 'wit' (seeing resemblances) and 'judgment' (seeing differences)" (17).

Before proceeding to analyze the epistemological functions of doubt and dialectic in Johnson's *Lives*, I cannot fail to mention that one Johnsonian of recent years has singled out and attacked the very idea of dialectical approaches to Johnson. James Battersby has argued that several recent critical studies are invalidated by "their common dialectical tendencies":

> [They] betray a common tendency to begin critical reasoning, not from some empirically distinguishable event or effect that it is then the business of criticism to explain in all its particularity in terms of necessary and sufficient conditions, but from some basic proposition or truth concerning, say, the modern point of view, Johnson's bifurcated sensibility, or his "thought." An abstract or general principle . . . is first established, and then particular passages or works are discussed in terms of their peculiar or specialized participation in the assumed proposition or principle.
> [*Rational Praise* 20]

Battersby is a bit of a dialectician himself when he goes so far as to divide the possible variations of dialectical approaches into three groups: those who see in Johnson "resolution without conflict," those who see "conflict without resolution," and those who see "conflict with resolution" (19).

I quote Battersby at length in order to indicate that, while his "destructive criticism" (19) is often quite accurate, his blanket objection to dialectical analysis is fallacious and misleading and should be set aside. What is wrong with the critical approaches he examines is not their dialectical pattern but their circularity; however, he lumps circularity and dialectic together, assuming that where dialectic appears, circularity is not far behind. He confuses dialectical schemata (which are merely devices for configuring thought) with critical procedures that are closed to logical verification and falsification. In failing to allow for the possibility of dialectical criticism open to falsification, he commits the very sort of circularity he attacks, finding only the sort of thing he set out to find.

I proceed by entertaining the possibility which Battersby disregards: that Johnson's bisociative patterns of thought may be precisely the sort of "empirically distinguishable . . . effect" Battersby requires and that, despite certain critics' "forcing" of the evidence, the dialectical tendencies in Johnson's writings are nevertheless conspicuous, significant, and worthy of analysis.

My study of Johnson's *Lives* begins at this point: the bisociative processes of comparison and contrast as they show Johnson's processes of probable judgment at work, not in the imposing of fictional patterns, but in the discovery and conveyance of biographical ones. Again and again Johnson asks us to place two entities side by side and to draw probable conclusions from the act of comparison; and the interest, I think, lies as much in the uncertainties, the problems inherent in probable argument, as in the conclusions Johnson reaches. Johnson can be intuitive, but he takes great pains to polarize the procedures of judging and evaluating and to bring them to the surface where they can be consciously scrutinized and transmitted.

The chapters of this book are designed to examine different aspects of this process of bisociative judgment. In "The 'Doubtfulness' of Johnson's *Lives*," I consider the psychological bases for Johnson's most consistent patterns of invoking doubt and uncer-

tainty. In "Johnson, Skepticism, and Biography," I examine the
doubts raised by skeptical philosophers, relating these to Johnson's manner of handling biographical testimony. In the remaining chapters I focus on individual biographies as they exemplify
aspects of Johnson's doubting tendencies; in addition, each of
these chapters attempts to focus on a current problem of critical
interpretation and evaluation.

In "Satire and Sympathy in the *Life of Savage*," I focus partly
on modern critics' tendencies to attribute the complex ambivalences of this biography to some unusual division of intention on
Johnson's part, when in fact emotional "dividedness" is just one
manifestation of Johnson's consistent—and highly effective—biographical practice. Johnson employs emotional response dialectically just as surely as he employs a dialectic of probable argument.

In "Johnson's Redaction of Hawkesworth's *Swift*," I analyze
Johnson's relationship to his chief predecessor and chief source in
Swiftian biography. Here I focus on Johnson's dialectical engagement with another biographer and with the problem of emphasis
in interpretation. Johnson's redaction of Hawkesworth shows him
doubting Hawkesworth's view throughout, but his *Life of Swift* is
far more than just responsive or refutative. In letting his doubts
guide him in recasting Hawkesworth's material, Johnson shows
some of his most characteristic strengths, even if the resulting
biography is his least fair. The distortions of the *Life of Swift* that
trouble modern Johnsonians may be at least in part attributable to
the complexities of Johnson's doubting relationship to his source
as well as his subject.

In "The Probable and the Marvelous in the *Life of Milton*," I
analyze Johnson's dialectical method of raising doubts as a corrective to a misguided sense of wonder and astonishment. The attempt to exemplify sound biographical practice leads Johnson to
engage in a constant opposition to Milton's biographers, even

while his own biographical methods and critical theories point up unresolved contradictions in his concept of the probable and the marvelous.

In "Judgment and the Art of Contrast in the *Life of Pope*," I try to show how Johnson's dialectical techniques work together in his finest biography. The greatness of the *Life of Pope* has been difficult for modern critics to analyze and describe, but a fuller awareness of the depth and consistency of Johnson's contrastive patterns may help to provide some terms adequate to describe his accomplishment. Finally, in my conclusion I attempt to relate Johnson's biographical practice to the perfecting of doubt as a creative instrument in the Enlightenment.

Alvin Kernan has summarized several decades of Johnson criticism:

> Two generations of Johnson scholars, re-examining the evidence, have gradually replaced the authoritarian Johnson with a much more complex Johnson, skeptical, deeply troubled in mind, mad at times, neurotic nearly always, radically doubtful of himself and of the social values he at the same time so stoutly defended. . . . the very force with which his truths are stated in speech or in writing, now directs attention to the near desperation of the effort and the unstable foundations on which the statements of truth are constructed. [117]

In a sense, criticism has for decades been deconstructing Johnson's body of work without using the jargon or the mannerisms of the deconstructionists. In analyzing Johnson's biographical skepticism, I intend to continue and to extend that line of development. The picture of Johnson the biographer that will emerge, I hope, is an image not merely of a writer who differs from himself but of a writer constantly alert to the usefulness of his own doubts. In Johnson's hands, doubt is a creative instrument, and dialectic is a way of achieving not a stalemate but a victory.

Two

The "Doubtfulness" of

Johnson's

Lives

An underlying source of power and coherence in Johnson's *Lives* is
his persistently skeptical approach to experience—his apparent
"scrupulosity" (which he defined in his *Dictionary* as "minute and
nice doubtfulness"). In all his writing and speaking, Johnson is a
doubter and an arguer to some extent, but one of his special tri-
umphs was to bring to life a new genre, biography, by giving it an
engrossingly skeptical and argumentative cast.

Of course, it was not the documentary uncertainties of biography that attracted Johnson to the form; he had little interest in
Boswellian adjustments of minute details in literary history. But
other kinds of uncertainty, other bases for doubt, attracted him
and even fascinated him. He welcomed opportunities to address
doubtful and problematic questions, for example, whenever they
could be resolved by armchair deliberation, by wide experience

The "Doubtfulness" of Johnson's
Lives

of human nature, or by wide knowledge of books. In the *Lives of the Poets* he recorded both the process and the product of his struggle with doubts—ranging from doubts about facts to doubts about the meaning and value of human lives.

Johnson's biographies embody a style of thinking about people: in moving repeatedly from doubt to resolution, they progress by means of the rhetorical back-and-forth pattern called dialectic, but behind the rhetorical shape lies a style of thinking, and behind that lies a style of character. More precisely, certain typical features of Johnson's rhetorical style derive from, or are at least paralleled by, certain features of his characterological style.

By "characterological style" I mean a characteristic set of "ways of thinking and perceiving, ways of experiencing emotion, modes of activity that are associated with various pathologies" (David Shapiro 1)—in Johnson's case, the pathology of obsessive-compulsive neurosis. I adopt the neutral term, "characterological style," partly to indicate my indebtedness to Ernest Becker and partly to avoid the pejorative connotations of Shapiro's term "neurotic style" (see Becker 47–66). Strictly speaking, the term "neurotic" denotes maladaptive behavior, whereas "characterological" refers more broadly to both maladaptive and adaptive behavior. In other words, "style" as a concept describing character applies not just to neurotic behaviors nor just to healthy ones but to features common to both. "Style," in this sense, is exactly the "something" that "characterizes" an individual at his sickest and at his healthiest.

Before turning to some of the healthier and more creative results of Johnson's doubting cast of mind, one should recognize that there was a pathological side; he was a pathological doubter. In particular, one thinks of a cluster of doubts that recurrently made Johnson miserable: hypochondriacal doubts, doubts about his sanity, about his self-worth, about his eventual fate at the

hands of a stern God. At the center of all this doubting was "the
fierce sense and exacting sense of self-demand" that Bate discusses
so well:

> Arthur Murphy . . . said that there was "danger" for Johnson in
> indolence; for "his spirits, not employed abroad, turned with in-
> ward hostility against himself. His reflections on his own life and
> conduct were always severe; and, wishing to be immaculate, he
> destroyed his own peace by unnecessary scruples." And in John-
> son's own moral writing, which often anticipates psychoanalysis,
> he was to show—in a way close to modern psychiatry—how
> much of the misery of mankind comes from the inability of indi-
> viduals to think well of themselves, and how much envy and
> other evils spring from this. One of the aims of biography, he
> thought, was to inquire into this—to learn how a man was made
> happy; not how he lost the favour of his prince, but how he be-
> came discontented with himself. [*Samuel Johnson* 121–22]

The characterological style of the compulsive is shaped by the
perpetual discontent of excessive self-demands and by defensive
strategies directed against those demands. As David Shapiro describes it, the life of the typical compulsive (and Johnson is truly
typical in this respect) "is characterized by a more or less continuous experience of tense deliberateness, sense of effort, and of trying" (31). The compulsive nags himself, even about what he
should be feeling; he tries to direct even his own emotions. Instead of following impulses, he tries to control them. He is therefore "cut off from the sources that normally give willful effort its
direction" (37). That is, his life is "driven"; he has "the self-
awareness of a person who is working under pressure with a stop-
watch in hand" (37). Furthermore, readers who have been struck
by the violent contrast between Johnson's frequently dogmatic
assertiveness in conversation and the anguished uncertainties of

The "Doubtfulness" of Johnson's
Lives

his private journal will note that Shapiro describes the compulsive style in terms that help explain the psychodynamics of
doubt: the obsessive-compulsive "is characterized symptomati-
cally by two outstanding features: doubt and uncertainty, on the
one hand, and dogma, on the other. Psychoanalysis has already
dissolved this paradox by demonstrating a significant relationship
between the two. Dogma arises in order to overcome doubt and
ambivalence and to compensate for them" (51).

Although Johnson relished certain kinds of technical-indicator
procedures for resolving uncertainties (his fondness for calculations comes to mind), he was notably free from the narrowness,
rigidity, and lack of sense of proportion characteristic of compulsive neurosis; on the contrary, his breadth of attention and the
subtlety of his sense of moral proportion were his characteristic
strengths, suggesting that in Johnson there was an adaptive side
to compulsivity. Johnson's doubts enriched, rather than impoverished, his experience. This applies perhaps even to some of
the miseries that resulted from his compulsive "scruples" and
doubts. Johnson was an anguished doubter, a strenuous believer,
in an age that was exploring the grounds for doubt and belief in
science and religion. Perhaps doubt and the need to push against
doubt made Johnson the universally curious and inquisitive genius that he was. Certainly it made him a sort of representative
man of his era.

It would be misleading to portray Johnson as some miraculous
prodigy of shrewd skepticism. He could be humanly credulous.
It has been shown that he perpetuated many biographical errors,
that for the *Lives of the Poets* he did little research in the modern
sense, and that his astonishing memory could sometimes fail him.
Yet how often in the *Lives* Johnson expresses skeptical doubts
about his evidence. If he is not writing from "common fame and a
very slight personal knowledge," he has learned something merely

"by hearsay" (3:400, 78); if he is lucky, he has found some "few memorials" of his subject, but sometimes he has "sought intelligence . . . but [has] not obtained it" (2:257). It is certainly fair to say that Johnson is scrupulous, compared to most of the life writers of his day, in incorporating evaluation of sources as part of his biographical method. In the lives of Milton, Addison, and Swift, not to mention many of the shorter and less familiar lives, he turns aside to evaluate his sources' reliability. (See 1:84, 201–2, 222; 2:18, 37, 116, 312–13; 3:1, 281.) He repeatedly reminds the reader that his information is partial, vague, confused, or contradictory—and then shows how one can sift through such material to arrive at some probable version of the truth.

Flattering biographies always prompt Johnson's expressions of doubt. He repeatedly displays his antipanegyrical conception of biography by mocking or dryly undercutting his sources, even those from which he borrows extensively. Sprat's biography of Cowley, for example, he calls "a funeral oration rather than a history" (1:1), while Temple's flattering portrait of Gray, which Johnson quotes at length, is preceded by a droll disclaimer: Johnson says he is "as willing as his warmest well-wisher to believe it true" (3:429). (Here Johnson wants to alert the reader to the superlatives, to awaken the reader's doubts—but without seeming uncharitable. He uses irony to imply that even a well-wisher would be suspicious of praise so excessive.) In places—most conspicuously, in the *Life of Milton*—Johnson's exercises in antipanegyric verge on biographer baiting. He seems amused by the hagiographical reverence brought to the Milton industry and determined to pillory the biographers. He insists that his will not be another of the "honeysuckle lives" of Milton (1:84n1).

An interesting example of Johnson's vigorous and debunking skepticism occurs in his treatment of Milton's work habits. Here is the topic for doubtful consideration: whether Milton worked in great bursts of creativity or not. Johnson finally rejects the notion of Milton's working by fits. Why? Partly because his biographer, Richardson, too openly flatters Milton and too often shows his "wish to find Milton discriminated from other men" (1:138). It is not stretching the point too far to say that Johnson chooses to quote Richardson on this subject partly to exhibit the folly of credulous biographers:

> Richardson, who seems to have been very diligent in his enquiries, but discovers always a wish to find Milton discriminated from other men, relates, that "he would sometimes lie awake whole nights, but not a verse could he make; and on a sudden his poetical faculty would rush upon him with an *impetus* or *oestrum*, and his daughter was immediately called to secure what came. At other times he would dictate perhaps forty lines in a breath, and then reduce them to half the number." [1:138]

The effect of this passage is mildly but unmistakably comic. One imagines a Johnsonian snort of derision after "*impetus* or *oestrum*"— an impression reinforced by Johnson's outburst of learned diction in the sentence that immediately follows: "These bursts of light and involutions of darkness, these transient and involuntary excursions and retrocessions of invention." (The etymological meanings associated with *oestrum*, incidentally, by which Richardson means poetic frenzy, nicely fit Johnson's portrayal of Milton as unmanly, here as a woman in imaginary heat or in the throes of parturition— the latter impression deriving from the summoning of Milton's daughter "to secure what came.") But while the controlling intention may be comic, Johnson is also demonstrating "practical biography" by enacting doubts and ways of reasoning about them. He enacts resistance to the credulity displayed by Milton's biographers and, it is implied, by Milton himself, who believed he experienced fits of inspiration.

The Philosophical
Biographer

It has often been noted that one of the unifying themes of the
Lives is the writer's susceptibility to flattery, deception, and self-
deception. In his treatment of previous biographers, Johnson sets
up a contrapuntal expression of the same theme: biographers are
easily taken in by the "desire to propagate a wonder" or by "common topicks of falsehood" (1:3, 132). The typical Johnsonian tone
is bracing, debunking, as he sweeps away the subjects' self-decep-
tions and the biographers' distortions. A skeptical conception of
biography thus emerges by practice rather than by precept as
Johnson grapples with a set of doubts associated with the form,
ranging from arguable questions of evidence, to unanswerable
questions about human motivation: "actions are visible, though
motives are secret" (1:15).

Doubt shapes not only his conception of the genre but also the
structure of individual lives. The *Life of Milton* is an example but
perhaps an unfortunate one, since it is so slanted. In it, the pattern of dialectical engagement with previous biographers is "rhetorical" in the poorest sense. Johnson has already made up his
mind about Milton; so his skeptical and argumentative stance is
abrasive and finally unfair.

But when Johnson is at his best, as in the *Life of Savage* and the
Life of Pope, one forms the impression that his skeptical manner of
approaching the subject is subordinated to an intense curiosity, a
genuinely doubting engagement in questions of interpreting and
evaluating individual human lives. (A similar dialectic of thought
and feeling marks both these *Lives*, separated by thirty-five
years—evidence, if any is needed, for Johnson's consistency.) At
his best, Johnson involves the reader in the process of puzzling
out the meanings of a life. The *Life of Savage* in particular has
attracted much puzzled critical commentary because of the peculiar seesaw movement of emotion embodied in its structure. Just
when Johnson has reached a pathetic low point, he invites a comic

response, while at moments of high comedy, pathos reappears; thus in the *Life of Savage* one feeling is always canceling or modifying the feeling that precedes it. In analytic terms, his affective style parallels his cognitive style; that is, doubts about *how to feel* are as important to him as doubts about *what to think*. And in some of the *Lives of the Poets*—the *Life of Savage* is the best example—affective ambiguity amounts to a controlling structural principle.

As one moves down the scale, from Johnson's conception of biography, to the design of individual lives and passages within those lives, and finally to Johnson's syntax and imagery, it becomes easier with the smaller units to see that Johnson's affective-cognitive style is perhaps based on a similar perceptual style. His manner of enacting doubts about his thoughts and feelings seems to be based on a manner of doubting his very perceptions. This point can best be seen from his syntax and imagery.

Syntactical patterns of antithesis are often rhetorical embodiments of dialectical habits of thought. Since every assertion implies a negation, the connection between antithesis and dialectic is self-evident: "The more peculiar and complex the affirmation the more it may need the emphasis of negation, the more negation itself, elaborated in its own aspects, may become a relevant and parallel meaning, until which is superior and which is subordinate is hardly to be told, rather the two as a pair of reflecting, reciprocal movements are the true theme of the discourse" (Wimsatt, *Prose Style* 38). Precisely this doubtful interplay between affirmation and negation—and precisely this ambiguity about which element is subordinate and which is superior—characterizes Johnson's syntax and paragraph structure as well as his affective-cognitive style: "To Johnson's frequent use of major antitheses, and to his incessant scoring of paragraphs with all kinds of minor and implied antitheses, is due the abrupt, sectional character of his writing. It is put together with tight logic, it is eminently coherent and articulate, but it does not flow. . . . Logical progression is of that sort; it moves by distinctions, which are antitheses, which may be jerks" (Wimsatt, *Prose Style* 46–47). This quality of Johnson's style has long been noticed; in his *Life of Johnson*, John Hawkins described Johnson's style as possessing "a certain even-handed justice that leaves the mind in a strange perplexity. . . . [Johnson] frequently raises an edifice, which appears founded and supported to resist any attack; and then, with the next stroke, annihilates it, and leaves the vacuity he found" (quoted by Wimsatt, *Prose Style* 47).

As Bate observes, the writing of pro-and-con arguments in the *Parliamentary Debates* trained Johnson in prompt dialectical habits of thought, embodied in a "powerful back-and-forth movement, where a thing is immediately given its due, stabilized with permanence of phrase, and then qualified with another position given equal justice" (*Samuel Johnson* 207).

This constant dialectical give-and-take characterizes both Johnson's style of thinking about a subject and his style of expressing emotion. He seems as ready to doubt the validity of his own emotional responses as he is ready to doubt the truth of an argument or the reliability of a source, so there are rapid tonal shifts when one attitude gives way to another.

For Johnson, it seems that even objects of perception may be involved in the process of turning into something else. Consider a visual analogy: in the gesture known as the double-take, one looks away, doubts, and looks again—perhaps expecting to find the object transformed. Favorite perceptual terms in the Johnsonian lexicon suggest just such a process: "blaze, clouded, confused, diminished, gleams, glittering, magnified, misty, obscure, phantom." Such words relating to visual indistinctness, as well as words which subliminally suggest acts of visual perception

("show," "seem," "illustrate," "observe"), are important to Johnson
in that they make concrete the abstract interplay of doubt and
belief.[1]

The visual double-take, in fact, can be seen as the simple perceptual model for Johnson's other, more complex forms of verbal
doubting. Just as his structuring of paragraphs and sentences sets
up patterns of scrupulous dialectical reversal, in which assertion
is followed by doubt and counterassertion, so his favorite visual
images and metaphors suggest a pattern of double-take: look,
doubt, and look again. Experience is dangerous. One had better
check one's perceptions—scrupulously. In the famous opening
lines of *The Vanity of Human Wishes*, the terrifying uncertainties of
human life are expressed in precisely such visual terms, in language densely and scrupulously qualified:

> Then say how Hope and Fear, Desire and Hate,
> O'er spread with Snares the clouded Maze of Fate,
> Where wav'ring Man, betray'd by vent'rous Pride,
> To tread the dreary Paths without a guide,
> As treach'rous Phantoms in the Mist delude,
> Shuns fancied Ills, or chases airy Good.
>
> [*Poems* 31]

When writing about doubts and uncertainties in the *Lives*,
Johnson habitually uses visual metaphors of darkness and brightness. Either truth is clouded, veiled, or obscured by darkness, or
it is hidden by glare, brilliance, and glitter. These metaphors of
darkness and brightness, with their implied double-takes, often
carry the skeptical and Swiftian implication that first impressions
are pleasing, while closer examination will reveal faults and bring
disappointment. Johnson notes, for example, that Congreve's *The
Old Bachelor* seems to show knowledge of the world but that when
"more nearly examined" it is seen to be derivative (2:216). Aken-

side's images first dazzle, then disappoint: "they are hidden . . . by a 'Veil of Light'; they are forms fantastically lost under superfluity of dress" (3:417). Gray's poetic ornamentation is striking at first, but "the images are magnified by affectation," and the odes "are marked by glittering accumulations of ungraceful ornaments" (3:440). Johnson often links visual acuity and critical acumen, as when he suggests that some critics squint only to blind themselves: "Some hardy champions undertook to rescue them [Gray's odes] from neglect, and in a short time many were content to be shewn beauties which they could not see" (3:426). Johnson always seems to be amused by the spectacle of rationalized self-deception—here the critical fad, the mass hypnosis induced by a universal desire to be "in the know." He relishes a chance to display his own independent skepticism by showing that the emperor has no clothes.

In the critical sections of the *Lives*, Johnson habitually contrasts surface appearances with underlying substance—finding that the doctrines of Pope's *Essay on Criticism*, for example, are mere commonplaces "recommended by . . . a blaze of embellishment" or that Sheffield's work "sometimes glimmers, but rarely shines" after one has taken a "steady view" of it (3:244; 2:175). As a biographer evaluating his sources, Johnson expresses his doubts in similar visual terms. He observes that, in Sprat's biography of Cowley, "all is shewn confused and enlarged through the mist of panegyric"; similarly, Pope's letters are seen to "exhibit a perpetual and unclouded effulgence of general benevolence and particular fondness" (1:1; 3:206). The visual metaphors point up and make concrete the writers' delusions and self-delusions.

"Glare" functions as a metaphor for striking or extravagant characteristics, as in this comment on Rochester: "The glare of his general character diffused itself upon his writings. . . . This blaze of reputation is not yet quite extinguished; and his poetry still retains some splendour beyond that which genius has bestowed"

(1:222). If "glare" can represent the adventitious gleam imparted to a man's works by his character, it can also represent, more conventionally, the blaze of worldly success: in his prosperous years, Richard Savage used his social position "to take a nearer view" of the social elite, "to examine whether their merit was magnified or diminished by the medium through which it was contemplated; whether the splendour with which they dazzled their admirers was inherent in themselves, or only reflected on them by the objects that surrounded them" (2:371). In this example, one can see that the visual metaphor sometimes has a philosophical or scientific tone that appeals to Johnson; here he exploits that tone for gentle comic effect.

One final example will show even more clearly the "nice doubtfulness" of Johnson's characteristic style of perceiving, thinking, and feeling. In a poignant treatment of the theme of self-deception, Johnson first demonstrates the evident "fallacy and sophistication" of Pope's too consistently benevolent letters, but then he concludes that Pope deluded even himself into seeing his own letters as accurate self-portraits (3:207). Rather than attack this self-deception, however, Johnson uses it, in one of his characteristic reversals of tone and argument, to excuse Pope from the charge of hypocrisy:

> To charge those favourable representations, which men give of their own minds, with the guilt of hypocritical falsehood, would show more severity than knowledge. The writer commonly believes himself. . . . It is easy to awaken generous sentiments in privacy; to glow with benevolence when there is nothing to be given. While such ideas are formed they are felt, and self-love does not suspect the gleam of virtue to be the meteor of fancy.
> [3:207–8]

As F. W. Hilles has noted, "Johnson first wrote: 'self-love does not suspect them to be the meteors of fancy'" ("The Making of

The Life of Pope" 283). Hilles suggests that Johnson revised "them" to read "the gleam of virtue" with the aim of improving the sentence's cadence, but actually the revision produces several other, more significant types of improvement. For one thing, there is a more scrupulous parallelism in the revised version (gleam : virtue; meteor : fancy). More important, the increased visualization requires the reader to complete the perceptual gesture of double-take, from pleasing gleam of virtue to similar but disappointing meteor of fancy. And whereas in the original version the antecedent of "them" is "ideas," in the carefully modified revision it is a *particular* idea (virtue) and not even the idea itself but its mere appearance, its *gleam.* The much strengthened second version of this sentence shows the characteristic Johnsonian style, in which congruity and depth of implication are achieved through psychological patterns of response resembling the double-take, and the revision illustrates how Johnson's "second thoughts" work at the perceptual, cognitive, and affective levels simultaneously. The refinement of thought and feeling derives from a characteristic way of doubting evidence, even the evidence of one's own senses.

If doubting in its various forms is a pervasive characterological modality in Johnson's writings, the question remains: Why should this be so? Images of darkness, cloudiness, and obscurity often seem to represent some of Johnson's deepest terrors—terror of losing his sanity or the related but milder fear of losing his ability to perceive accurately and reliably. Against such fears Johnson erects his characterological armor, double-checking experience, structuring his sentences and paragraphs in dialectical equipoise in order to reassure himself that he is master of his own perceptions and judgments.

This scrupulosity, by which I especially mean Johnson's habitually skeptical, argumentative, and dialectical manner of approaching human experience, appeared everywhere in his work

The "Doubtfulness" of Johnson's
Lives

but especially in the writing of the *Lives of the Poets*, where it may have functioned as a defense against more specific anxieties. Biographical writing required Johnson to shape and manipulate doubtful material in the service of moral truth, and it challenged him by placing him behind the judgment bench. Thus he held his anxiety in check by alternately playing the roles of prosecuting and defending attorneys. Perhaps partly to assuage his deep-rooted terror of being judged harshly, he tried to write lives scrupulously and fairly. Or one could say that a dialectic of thought and feeling, embodied in various characteristic "ways of doubting," was one crucial means by which Johnson wrote magisterial, if not judicial, lives.

Distrust is a necessary qualification of a student of history.

SAMUEL JOHNSON

Three

Johnson, Skepticism,

and Biography

Whatever the psychological basis for Johnson's biographical skepticism might have been, its ultimate philosophical purpose was the education of the reader's faculty of judgment. The process of reading Johnson's biographical writings is an educational exercise in doubt and uncertainty because his rhetoric constantly forces us to suspend our judgment as we weigh dialectically opposed versions of the truth; he draws us into the process of skeptically comparing alternatives and evaluating probabilities.

His underlying biographical skepticism derives from a variety of sources, including the "constructive skepticism" of the seventeenth-century Christian apologists, the scientific epistemologies of Locke and Bacon, and the critical skepticism of Pierre Bayle.[1] Johnson's skeptical manner is a form of philosophical dialectic, a way of juxtaposing probabilities and forcing us to choose. He used it to keep his inferential procedures visible, as though he wanted us to *see* him judging probabilities, testing the limits of biographical inference.

Since the mathematical theory of probability sprang into being suddenly in the seventeenth century, some historians have

32

suggested that the very idea of probable truth may be as recent. But there were in fact older traditions of "the probable," and as Douglas Patey has argued, neoclassical literary criticism was essentially a working out of this traditional probabilism, a "theory of probable signs" which saw each work of literature as a system of signs pointing back to their causes (88). Thus the neoclassical literary work in its very conception embodied patterns of probable inference. The writer's task in character portrayal, for instance, was to find probable signs—actions and words—appropriate to a particular character type; from these probable signs the reader was to infer character. Such pervasive Augustan features as the inset story may have resulted from the influence of this theory of probable signs; in Patey's view, the inset story is a paradigmatic exercise in probable judgment (197).

Patey focuses strictly on fictional narrative, but his analysis has some interesting implications for biography. In a fiction, the neoclassical parts of the literary work—moral, fable, episodes, and so on—are created by the poet in accordance with decorums. In biography, however, the raw material is largely "given," so that in supplying a moral or in selecting episodes, a biographer is working inferentially as well as creatively. (Although the fictional work also embodies inferences, the nonfiction writer is uniquely bound by the givenness of the material.) For a morally earnest biographer such as Johnson, then, the new form may have held a special attraction: its requirement that the biographer be constantly involved in making paradigmatic inferences for his reader.

One of Johnson's distinguishing excellences as a biographer is that he keeps this inferential process visible, so that we constantly see him engaged in the evaluation of probabilities. Most narrowly, this takes the form of a dialectic in which Johnson juxtaposes two probable interpretations of a single sign, but dialectic has broader ramifications in his biographical technique; he is a master at exploiting the dialectical oppositions inherent in the rhetoric of biography. Doubt and belief, objective fact and subjective interpretation, omission and inclusion, distance and involvement, judgment and the withholding of judgment—these are but a few of the doubtful polarities that are the biographer's stock in trade, and Johnson uses them to make biography a model exercise in judgment.

As a genre, biography entails a number of uncertainties. What does it mean to "know" another person? If it is difficult sometimes to understand our own motives, actions, and emotions, how well can we understand those of another person? "In estimating the pain or pleasure of any particular state, every man, indeed, draws his decisions from his own breast, and cannot with certainty determine, whether other minds are affected by the same causes in the same manner. Yet by this criterion we must be content to judge, because no other can be obtained" (Yale *Works* 2:493). Johnson characteristically resolves such doubts "commonsensically," by suggesting that there is a degree of certainty appropriate to each sphere in life and that it is vain to wish for more certainty than experience allows. As he writes in his review of *An Account of the Conduct of the Duchess of Marlborough*, "distrust is a necessary qualification of a student of history. Distrust quickens his discernment of different degrees of probability, animates his search after evidence, and, perhaps, heightens his pleasure at the discovery of truth; for truth, though not always obvious, is generally discoverable" (*Works* [1825] 6:5–6).

When dealing with uncertain testimony, Johnson tends to think along lines laid down by Locke and the constructive skeptics of the seventeenth century, authorities on judging probable evidence. In evaluating testimony, Johnson displays his most consistent skepticism and his most consistent criteria for evaluating biographical truth claims. Although these criteria are nowhere systematically set forth in Johnson's writings, they can be ascertained by "mapping" Johnson's expressions of doubt and his ways of resolving those doubts. But first it is necessary to understand the complex relationship between Johnson the biographer and Johnson the student of the religious, philosophical, and general skepticism of his era.

Some students of eighteenth-century literature might object to the use of the term "skepticism" in characterizing Johnson's thought because they associate the term with an inverted dogmatism that denies the possibility of genuine knowledge. Others might object that "skepticism" connotes lack of Christian faith. The connotations of "skepticism" are wrong for Johnson on both counts. But despite Johnson's rejection of the more extreme forms of skeptical doubt, his manner of sifting historical and biographical testimony shows everywhere the influence of constructive skepticism; furthermore, his methods as a biographer were motivated by, and were modulated by, his reaction to the philosophical and religious skepticisms of his day.

We should distinguish between several historically interrelated meanings of the word "skepticism." Most narrowly, the word has come to mean "unbelief with regard to the Christian religion" (*Oxford English Dictionary*). More broadly, "skepticism" can mean doubt about whether there is a God. More broadly still, "skepticism" can mean the opinion that real knowledge of any kind is or may be unattainable; this is "philosophical skepticism."[2] Finally, "skepticism" in the broadest sense denotes "disposition to doubt or incredulity in general" (*Oxford English Dictionary*). I follow Phillip Harth in using the term to denote the methodical application of doubt as part of the process of inquiry (Harth 1–31).

For Johnson himself, the terms "skeptic" or "skeptical" almost invariably connote religious unbelief. Even when in his *Dictionary* he defines "skeptick" in the broader, philosophical sense as "one who doubts, or pretends to doubt of every thing," three of the four illustrative quotations actually refer to religious skepticism. "Skeptical" is "doubtful; pretending to universal doubt." "Skepticism" is "universal doubt; pretence or profession of universal doubt." As Robert DeMaria observes, "skepticism in general, like other codified philosophies, is an object of scorn in the *Dictionary.*"[3]

Johnson's own usage of the word "sceptic" (and its derivatives) in the *Lives* is usually pejorative. He describes Addison's religion as "neither weakly credulous nor wantonly sceptical" (2:149), and in the *Life of Milton* he suggests that, "if every sceptick in theology may teach his follies, there can be no religion" (1:108). In the *Life of Gray* he notes Gray's disapproval of "scepticism and infidelity" (2:63), while Garth's supposed conversion to Catholicism prompts a quotation from Lowth to the effect that "there is less distance than is thought between scepticism and popery, and that a mind wearied with perpetual doubt willingly seeks repose in the bosom of an infallible church" (2:63).

Johnson's definitions and uses of the term suggest that he saw all skeptical habits of thought as tending to some degree toward religious skepticism and that he saw religious skepticism as a sign of intellectual irresponsibility and outright deception. He also perceived the close psychological and historical connections between skepticism and dogmatism; one of the illustrative quotations under his definition of "skeptick" gives "skeptick" and "dogmatist" as antonyms, but his remarks on Garth show his awareness that "perpetual doubt" can feed the hunger for dogmatic infallibility. The remark on "scepticism and popery" also suggests that he was aware of the long tradition of Counter-Reformation uses of skeptical arguments in Catholic apologetics.

As a historical movement, philosophical skepticism influenced Johnson more through its effect upon scientific epistemology and seventeenth-century religious controversy than through the writings of his contemporaries or of earlier continental skeptics. He apparently read the Renaissance skeptics with little sympathy. In the opening lecture of part 2 of the Vinerian lectures, for instance, he refers to Montaigne as an "ingenious but whimsical French author" (McAdam 107). Of Johnson's attitude toward the important skeptics of seventeenth-century France—Naudé, Patin, Marandé, Le Vayer, Gassendi, La Peyrère, Sorbière—we know very little. He read Gassendi's biography of Peiresc, and he owned Gassendi's collected works (Boswell 2:521n; Greene, *Library* 86, 60). Johnson read Glanvill's *Scepsis Scientifica*—he quoted from it in the *Dictionary*—and he certainly knew of Sorbière, if only by way of Sorbière's preface to Gassendi or Sprat's *Observations on Sorbière's Voyage into England*.[4]

Rather than deriving from specific philosophical influences, Johnson's skeptical patterns of thought were conscious dialectical stratagems which he assimilated from a centuries-long tradition of skeptical argument. Revived in the Renaissance and variously modified in religious, scientific, and philosophical controversies over a period of two hundred years, skepticism in fact influenced Johnson indirectly in so many ways that we must be careful in disentangling the lines of influence.

The philosophical skepticism of the ancient world was embodied mainly in the writings of Cicero and Sextus Empiricus. Rediscovered and published in the sixteenth century, the writings of Empiricus immediately played a part in two parallel controversies. In the philosophical-scientific realm, skeptical arguments were instrumental in the evolution of the new science's empirical epistemology. In the moral-religious realm, skeptical arguments were employed in the Rule of Faith controversy revolving around the uncertainty of a criterion of truth in Christian belief.

Religious apologists, whether Catholic or Protestant, found skeptical arguments useful in support of faith. Since all knowledge is uncertain, they argued, this general uncertainty gives us all the more reason for accepting the best-attested religious truths on faith. The constructive skeptics argued that in a subject as vital as religion, one should stop short of unreasonable doubt. Johnson liked this "commonsensical" way of resolving uncertainty.

The trouble is, a skeptical attack upon the grounds for skepticism merely gives rise to another basis for argument: What criterion distinguishes reasonable from unreasonable doubt? Such an argument about a truth criterion requires another criterion to solve it, and the Pyrrhonian method of skeptical argument deriving from Sextus Empiricus refuses to grant such a criterion.

Such was the logical impasse created by the problem of truth criteria in the centuries-long Reformation debate over the "Rule of Faith," or criterion of religious knowledge. Luther skeptically questioned papal authority and proposed a new criterion: what our consciences compel us to believe upon reading Scripture is true. In reply, Erasmus gave skeptical reasons for remaining Catholic. Pyrrhonian arguments for and against religious beliefs became standard weapons of the Reformation and the Counter-Reformation, especially in France, where Pyrrhonism was used to attack the Calvinists' use of "inner persuasion" as the Rule of Faith.

A similar use of skepticism in support of religious belief emerged among the Anglican apologists and English scientists of the seventeenth century, who met the challenge of Pyrrhonism by formulating a commonsensical approach to truth criteria. Stillingfleet, Chillingworth, and Tillotson are the main exemplars of this line of thought, and they number among the authors whom Richard Popkin called the "constructive skeptics" of the seventeenth century, the "divines and others of the last century" to whom, John Hawkins said, Johnson "owed his excellence as a writer" (see Yale *Works* 3:xxxiii). Johnson follows their lead in applying skeptical doubt constructively, seeing it as a temporary stage in the process of arriving at probable truth.

Johnson, Skepticism, and
Biography

William Chillingworth's *The Religion of Protestants* was an early English adaptation of the views expressed by Castellio (*De arte dubitandi*) and Grotius (*De veritate religionis christianae*), an author Johnson struggled to read at age ten, who tried to show that it is impossible to attain complete certainty in religion and that consequently we need to be content with reasonable degrees of probability in religious matters. In the writings of Chillingworth and Tillotson, as well as in those of such apologists for the new science as Wilkins, Glanvill, Boyle, Locke, and Newton, "common sense about every day affairs is made the basis for settlement of perplexities about religion" (Van Leeuwen xiii). This common-sense mitigation of skepticism was based on the idea that "there are several levels of certainty ranging from absolute certainty to mere probability, each determined by a particular kind of evidence, and that an exact proportion must be maintained between evidence and certainty" (Van Leeuwen 14).

Because their central concern was the question of evidences for the Christian faith, and because such key evidences as miracles and prophecies derive from historical testimony, Chillingworth and Tillotson especially tended to concentrate on evaluating degrees of certainty in questions of testimony. Their criteria for evaluating testimony, deriving from ancient rhetorical canons for evaluating witnesses' reliability (Patey 7), evolved into those of Locke, who enumerated six: the number, integrity, and skill of witnesses, their purpose, the internal and external consistency of the circumstances related, and the presence or absence of contradictory testimony. Locke also shared the tendency of the "constructive skeptics" to apply skeptical and probabilistic reasoning to questions of morality and religion; one of his arguments for toleration is the typically skeptical one that, since religious questions are often questions of probability, we should tolerate each other's views. Johnson's familiarity with skeptical patterns of thought certainly owed much to his acquaintance with these seventeenth-century constructive skeptics; in particular, we know that his interest in the question of evidences for the Christian faith "continued to be one of his primary intellectual concerns until the final days of his life" (Walker, "Evidences" 41).

His most famous remarks on the subject of Christian evidences and skeptical doubt occurred in a conversation with Boswell on July 14, 1763:

> Talking of those who denied the truth of Christianity, he said, "It is always easy to be on the negative side. If a man were to deny that there is salt upon the table, you could not reduce him to an absurdity. Come, let us try this a little further. I deny that Canada is taken, and I can support my denial by pretty good arguments. The French are a much more numerous people than we; and it is not likely that they would allow us to take it. 'But the ministry have assured us, in all the formality of the Gazette, that it is taken.'—Ay, but these men have still more interest in deceiving us. They don't want that you should think the French have beat them, but that they have beat the French. Now suppose you should go over and find that it is really taken, that would only satisfy yourself; for when you come home we will not believe you. We will say, you have been bribed.—Yet, Sir, notwithstanding all these plausible objections, we have no doubt that Canada is really ours. Such is the weight of common testimony. How much stronger are the evidences of the Christian religion?" [Boswell 1:428]

Johnson uses skeptical arguments constructively in this famous passage. He refers to sense impressions as a criterion ("salt upon the table") to show that even the most certain of sense impressions may be subjected to unreasonable doubt; he then shifts to a question of testimony, where doubt may more reasonably be entertained; he impugns the number and the integrity of witnesses; and he triumphantly and commonsensically dismisses

Johnson, Skepticism, and
Biography

these grounds for doubt. He argues elsewhere that "we have as strong evidence for the miracles . . . as the nature of the thing admits" (Boswell 1:444–45). In using common sense as a criterion, and in evaluating levels or degrees of probability, Johnson follows in the footsteps of the constructive skeptics. In fact, as Robert G. Walker has noted, this argument probably derives from a similar argument put forth by Tillotson in his *The Rule of Faith* (Walker, "Credibility" 254–55). The idea that the degree of assent should be proportioned to the degree of evidence's credibility "was a keystone of seventeenth-century Anglican apologetics" (Walker, "Evidences" 33).

Like many of his contemporaries, Johnson believed that the really essential truths of the Christian religion are clear, understandable, and well attested:

> For revealed religion, he said, there was such historical evidence, as, upon any subject not religious, would have left no doubt. Had the facts recorded in the New Testament been mere civil occurrences, no one would have called in question the testimony by which they are established; but the importance annexed to them, amounting to nothing less than the salvation of mankind, raised a cloud in our minds, and created doubts unknown upon any other subject. . . .
>
> With regard to evidence, Dr. Johnson observed that we had not such evidence that Caesar died in the Capitol, as that Christ died in the manner related. [Hill, *Johnsonian Miscellanies* 2:384]

Johnson felt that the Christian faith rested upon credible historical evidence; thus he could use skeptical doubt defensively, showing that *excessive* doubts were disproportionate to the weight of testimony.

This commonsense solution to the problem of religious doubt seems to have satisfied Johnson. Whatever his religious uncertainties, they seem to have related more to the question of his own spiritual worth than to the question of faith. Indeed, Johnson regarded extreme skepticism in philosophy and religion as downright pathological; his *Rambler* 95 is a portrait of a skeptic Johnson calls Pertinax, who searches "not after proofs, but objections" (Yale *Works* 4:146). This habit of radical doubt leads him into psychopathological confusion from which he barely recovers. As Chester Chapin observes, "Johnson considers radical skepticism a mental disease, something quite different from that creative distrust which leads to the discovery of truth" ("Common Sense" 63).

In addition to this constructive skepticism that sought a commonsensical solution to the problem of the "Rule of Faith" and concerned itself particularly with the historical reliability of the "evidences" for the faith, there was another skeptical influence upon Johnson. This was the epistemology deriving from Bacon and Locke that sought to resolve the problem of truth criteria in the physical sciences: if words and ideas are built upon sense data, and if sense data are unreliable, then the language and concepts of science are doubtful, too. Empiricist epistemology had to justify itself against the age-old problem posed by the skeptics: How can we ever know the true inner workings of nature when perception touches only nature's surfaces?

One answer was Bacon's view of human knowledge, which took into account the "idols" of human language and perception in order "to reconstitute knowledge on a basis of certainty."[5] In epistemology, Pyrrhonism threatened to undermine the claims of the new science by noting that, since our knowledge of phenomena is derived from potentially deceptive sense data, we can know only the outward manifestations of things, not their inner or essential natures. To Johnson, as to Bacon, the surest refutation of such doubts was the knowledge provided by the new science in its program of "ordered study, diligent observation and experimenta-

Johnson, Skepticism, and
Biography

tion" (Schwartz, *New Science* 70).[6] In Bacon perhaps he could see the empiricist's use of skeptical doubt as a means of reaching probable truth rather than as an evasion or rejection of all knowledge that falls short of certainty.

If Bacon was empiricism's advocate and exemplar, its theorist was Locke. From the constructive skeptics Locke adapted the notion of degrees of assent, correlating them with three levels of knowledge: intuitive knowledge, demonstrative knowledge, and opinion. Intuitive knowledge, in Locke's familiar argument, is based upon the immediate, intuitively perceived congruity of clear and distinct ideas; demonstrative knowledge is based upon linked series of such congruities; and opinion or judgment is based upon ideas whose congruity or incongruity is not immediately apparent. Locke's theory rescues empirical knowledge from the skeptics by assigning to the rational faculty of judgment the task of weighing probabilities where certainties are impossible.

Johnson habitually draws the distinction between demonstrative and probabilistic reasoning; he once commented characteristically that "the next degree of satisfaction to the attainment of certainty is the knowledge that certainty cannot be attained" (McAdam 98). Johnson's probabilism, like John Locke's, served to anchor his view of knowledge between the extremes of skepticism and dogmatism (Trowbridge, "Probability" 4–5), and his probabilism, like Locke's, derived many of its characteristic assumptions from constructive skepticism.

While Locke and the constructive skeptics helped to shape Johnson's style of thinking, an avowed skeptic helped Johnson find his manner of arguing: Pierre Bayle. Johnson's distinctive biographical persona is that of a Christian moralist who uses the tone of a radical skeptic, and this skeptical manner derives from Bayle. Johnson used *A General Dictionary, Historical and Critical* (1734–41), an English work based on Bayle, as a source in the

Lives of the Poets (Rogers 150), and he told Boswell, "Bayle's Dictionary is a very useful work for those who love the biographical part of literature, which is what I love most" (1:425). Scattered references to Bayle suggest that it was especially Bayle the biographer and critical historian that Johnson admired and emulated (see Boswell 1:285 and 5:287).

Johnson was Baylean, too, in his famous preference for factual genres—a "preference rooted in a respect for the authority of concrete fact and immediate observation" (Edinger 78). In a way, *Idler* 84 is a Baylean defense of historical criticism: "Certainty of knowledge not only excludes mistake, but fortifies veracity. What we collect by conjecture, and by conjecture only can one man judge of another's motives or sentiments, is easily modified by fancy or desire; as objects imperfectly discerned, take forms from the hope or fear of the beholder. But that which is fully known cannot be falsified but with reluctance of understanding, and alarm of conscience" (Yale *Works* 2:263). Biography was the perfect vehicle for the Baylean critical project: the establishment of the "fully known" upon the ruins of the falsified.

The biographies originally entitled *Prefaces, Biographical and Critical* are critical in still another, more important sense: Johnson's criticism, like Bayle's, facilitates a direct relationship between the reader's judgment and the text, and it thereby transfers authority from text to critical reader. Criticism in this broad sense, Jean Starobinski argues, defends human judgment against the "risk of disorder" entailed by the Renaissance's massive restoration of history, its "influx of information":

> Criticism (particularly as practiced by Pierre Bayle) discovers history not in the narration, but in the very act of situating such historical material as has been verified by the best available resources. The collection of evidence, the rejection of all opinions

adopted solely on the guarantee of a so-called trustworthy source, the battle against false conclusions, paralogisms whose theses are supported only by dogmatic tenets: such are some of the aspects of that extirpation of errors which constitutes the official intention of Bayle's *Dictionary*. [4]

Precisely such extirpation of errors, collation of evidence, rejection of opinions, and evaluation of testimony distinguish Johnson's *Lives* as *critical* biographies. Johnson's historical skepticism—more precisely, his constant attempt to employ that skepticism constructively—puts him in the Enlightenment critical tradition initiated by Bayle, who saw as the purpose of criticism the strengthening of the reader's independent judgment.

Johnson's skeptical approach to biography casts doubt upon Ira Bruce Nadel's argument that empiricism led to a "domination of fact" in biography until the "shaped, interpretative life" emerged in the nineteenth century (5, 7). Johnson's biographical skepticism functions to elicit the reader's participation in the weighing of evidence. At least in Johnson's hands, an inductive, empirical approach never led to that simplistic belief in "factual" biography which Nadel associates with empiricism (155). On the contrary, Johnson follows Bayle's example in constantly questioning the supposed "facts"; like Bayle, he uses doubts about "facts" as ways of engaging the reader's judgment.

Bayle defended the value of historical study by invoking the familiar principle of degrees of assent, arguing that probable conclusions should be valued according to the kind of certitude appropriate to them. He gave as an example of historical truth the sort of commonplace illustration that was constantly employed by the constructive skeptics: the well-attested truth that Caesar defeated Pompey. Skeptics usually argued that truth based on historical testimony was less certain than demonstrative truth, but

Bayle turns this notion around to argue for the superior credibility of historical fact—"not because . . . [fact] can be employed within the perspective of a broad historical narration based on the ensemble of verified facts, but because the critical act [of ascertaining factual truth] has a value of its own" (Starobinski 5). Bayle and Johnson part company here, since for Bayle "the criticism of factual errors becomes instrumental in a *general criticism*" that ultimately undermines theological discourse (Starobinski 6), while for Johnson critical thought serves to strengthen faith. But we should follow Margaret Wiley in distinguishing between skepticism as a product and skepticism as an active process of truth seeking by means of dialectical habits of thought (16–18). Johnson is vigorously skeptical in this latter sense, and much of his skepticism takes Bayle as its enabling precedent.

II

While the lines of skeptical influence upon Johnson may be complex, tangled, and elusive, their effects are clear and immediate. Epistemologically, Johnson is guided by an effective and consistent theory of historical inquiry, and the best way to see this point is to notice that he consistently applies constructively skeptical criteria to the evaluation of testimony in his masterpiece, the *Lives of the Poets*.

Deception and self-deception are such prevalent topics in the *Lives* that they become a consistent, controlling theme; skeptical doubt is a natural response for a writer so concerned with the ways in which we deceive ourselves and others. Boswell says that Johnson "was indeed so much impressed with the prevalence of falsehood, voluntary or unintentional, that I never knew any person who upon hearing an extraordinary circumstance told, discovered more of the *incredulus odi*. He would say with a significant

look and decisive tone, 'It is not so. Do not tell this again'"
(3:229).

Johnson's technique as a moralist-biographer is therefore always to enact doubt for us, teaching us by example to be on guard
against falsehood—for moral judgment depends upon a sense of
proportion in weighing probabilities, even to the point of a *nil
admirari* refusal to be impressed. "Wonders are willingly told and
willingly heard," Johnson writes, turning aside like Bayle in order
to show the necessity of being on guard against our constitutional
credulity, which he calls "the natural desire of man to propagate a
wonder" (*Lives* 3:172; 1:3). In one sense, "wonder" is the enemy of
morality itself, for Johnson remembers always that "we are affected only as we believe; we are improved only as we find something to be imitated or declined" (3:438). Instruction depends
upon credibility, and credibility depends upon a realistic sense of
what is morally possible.

Johnson's biographies are studded with references to "common topicks of falsehood" (1:132) propagated by biographers and
their subjects. Johnson's doubts are automatically stirred up
whenever a tale is too obviously of the sort that people *want* to
believe—to magnify their own importance, to gratify their malice
or envy, or just to make a good story. Milton's purported refusal
of a government post is suspect because "large offers and sturdy
rejections are among the most common topicks of falsehood"
(1:132). Similarly, Johnson dismisses the story of Dryden's being
bitterly upset by Prior's mockery of *The Hind and the Panther*.
Johnson attacks the story's credibility by making a comment on
human gullibility: "By tales like these is the envy raised by superior abilities every day gratified; when they are attacked, every
one hopes to see them humbled; what is hoped is readily believed,
and what is believed is confidently told" (2:182). Johnson is
amused to see that, for the sake of a good story, witty comments

are misattributed: "A pointed sentence is bestowed by successive transmission on the last whom it will fit" (2:171). He is wryly aware that anecdotes are often believed simply because they are satisfying: Milton saved Davenant's life, according to one anecdote, and later Davenant saved Milton's. Johnson comments: "Here is a reciprocation of generosity and gratitude so pleasing that the tale makes its own way to credit" (1:129). Johnson then demolishes the anecdote's credibility.

In addition to expressing doubts based upon general human credulity, Johnson frequently comments upon his uncertainty about the motives and feelings of his subjects. Often he shies away from analyzing motives explicitly, and he sometimes states the grounds for his doubts in categorical terms: "The fact is certain; the motives we must guess" (2:99). Again, comparing two sources whose analyses of motives disagree: "actions are visible, though motives are secret" (2:15).

Such uncertainties become especially pressing when determination of the subject's motives and feelings is essential to a full moral evaluation of him. An example is the ultimately unresolvable issue of Dryden's sincerity in his religious conversions. As a deductive premise Johnson proposes that a "conversion will always be suspected that apparently concurs with interest" (1:377); yet "one [that is, interest] may by accident introduce the other [that is, truth]" (1:378). Furthermore, we naturally "hope . . . that whoever is wise is also honest." "But," Johnson concludes, "enquiries into the heart are not for man; we must now leave him to his Judge" (1:378).

The common element in these instances of Johnson's uncertainty is the problematic relationship between action and motive, which is a form of uncertainty about the relationship of signs to the things they signify. Sometimes Johnson will discredit a piece of evidence by questioning the probability of the signs them-

Johnson, Skepticism, and
Biography

selves; thus a story about Addison's being upset about *Windsor Forest* is discredited because "the pain that Addison might feel it is not likely that he would confess" (3:106). On the other hand, when Johnson has reason to believe that a given action is a factual and reliable indication of his subject's feelings and motives, he says so. Some pages after the fairly elaborate analysis of Dryden's motives outlined above, Johnson refers to Dryden's subsequent action: "It is some proof of Dryden's sincerity in his second religion, that he taught it to his sons" (1:394). Similarly, Dryden's "frequent bursts of resentment give reason to suspect" that his critics and rivals disturbed his peace of mind (1:370).

Sometimes, as Robert Folkenflik has noted (*Samuel Johnson, Biographer* 74–77), Johnson presents a range of alternative motives which in effect engage the reader in the process of biographical interpretation: "Actuated therefore by zeal for Rome, or hope of fame, [Dryden] published *The Hind and the Panther*" (1:380). In the *Life of Thomson*, Johnson suggests that "Thomson's bashfulness, or pride, or some other motive perhaps not more laudable, withheld him" from acting in his own interest (3:290). Characteristically, Johnson presents his most unflattering analyses as series of alternatives or as uncertain surmises, a technique Leo Braudy has called the "epistemological doublet" because it skeptically calls attention to the uncertainties of historical interpretation.[7]

Perhaps the oddest, most amusing, and most effective example of Johnson's offering apparent alternatives in trying to determine his subject's feelings occurs in the *Life of Cowley*. Cowley sought happiness in retirement but "wisely went only so far from the bustle of life as that he might easily find his way back." Was he then happy? Johnson quotes a letter in which Cowley describes the miseries of his lying ill in the country. Johnson then concludes: "He did not long enjoy the pleasure or suffer the uneasiness of solitude, for he died at the Porch-house in Chertsey in

1667, in the 49th year of his age" (1:16–17). Johnson skillfully uses a variety of responses to the uncertainties of trying to understand another person's motives and feelings—from somber silence to careful analysis to tongue-in-cheek irony verging on black humor.

Johnson frequently questions the validity of his sources, and his biographical skepticism expresses itself most clearly in his concern with all of Locke's criteria for evaluating testimony. These are, to recapitulate briefly: the number, skill, and integrity of witnesses; the intentions of authors; internal and circumstantial evidence that testimony is doubtful; and contrary testimony. There is of course no way to prove conclusively that Johnson consciously had these in mind as he evaluated biographical testimony; almost anyone involved in trying to establish biographical truth is bound to invoke one or more of these criteria. But the integrity and consistency of Johnson's methods allow one to make at least a probable case for the idea that his biographical skepticism derives from Locke's views on testimony.

Although Johnson certainly commits and perpetuates biographical errors, he evaluates testimony scrupulously and is always eager to determine "the writer's means of information or character of veracity" (1:409). Sometimes Johnson employs "one of his favorite methods of adducing evidence, the *argumentum e silentio*" (Folkenflik, *Samuel Johnson, Biographer* 143), so that the very absence of testimony itself is treated as evidence: "Traditional memory retains no sallies of [Pope's] raillery nor sentences of observation, nothing either pointed or solid, either wise or merry," and so Johnson infers that Pope is unlikely to have excelled in conversation (3:201). When testimony is by its very nature conjectural and inconclusive, Johnson brands it as such in quasi-legal terms: "a crime that admits no proof, why should we believe?" (1:396) and "if accusation without proof be credited, who shall be innocent?" (1:398).

Johnson, Skepticism, and
Biography

Johnson often attacks the skill of the biographers whose writings he is using. Especially in the *Life of Milton*, one can sense Johnson's frustration in trying to reach the truth despite the biographers' hagiographical reverence and frequent incompetence. "This is another instance which may confirm Dalrymple's observation," Johnson observes at one point, " 'that whenever Burnet's narrations are examined, he appears to be mistaken' " (1:128).

Questions about the integrity of witnesses constantly arouse Johnson's skepticism. He is particularly on guard against evidence that witnesses are indulging in flattery, either of themselves or of others. Pope's letters, for example, are self-serving in the way they "exhibit a perpetual and unclouded effulgence of general benevolence and particular fondness."[8] Pope also liked to flatter himself by believing himself "important and formidable" (3:181), and he occasionally threatened self-importantly to write no more. Johnson comments mordantly: " 'There is nothing,' says Juvenal, 'that a man will not believe in his own favour.' Pope had been flattered till he thought himself one of the moving powers in the system of life. When he talked of laying down his pen, those who sat around him intreated and implored, and self-love did not suffer him to suspect that they went away and laughed" (3:153–54).

At its worst, self-flattery would seem to be morally harmless, though worthy of ridicule. But Johnson hates self-importance precisely because it leads to more serious distortions of the truth: "Falsehoods from which no evil immediately visible ensues, except the general degradation of human testimony, are very lightly uttered, and once uttered are sullenly supported" (2:213). Seemingly harmless distortions soon damage the self-flatterer's sense of moral proportion; thus Blackmore, though Johnson considered him "very honest," could "easily make a false estimate of his own importance: those whom their virtue restrains from deceiving

others are often disposed by their vanity to deceive themselves"
(2:240). From self-deception it is only a short step to more serious
folly: "He that is much flattered soon learns to flatter himself: we
are commonly taught our duty by fear or shame, and how can
they act upon the man who hears nothing but his own praises?"
(3:46). Johnson carries his moralizing treatment of self-flattery fur-
thest in the *Life of Halifax*, which actually ends with a five-para-
graph "moral essay" on the seductive appeal of flattery and self-
flattery, so that Halifax becomes a warning example of the folly of
believing those who sing our praises (2:46–47).

Both in theory and in practice Johnson resists his predecessors'
conception of biography as extended narrative in praise of an exemplary subject; he detests a life written as "a funeral oration
rather than a history," distorted by "all the partiality of friendship" (1:1; 2:1). He questions biographical testimony whenever it
bears signs of an overestimation of the subject: Warburton gulli-
bly believes Pope stopped writing satires because of his "despair
of prevailing over the corruption of his time" (3:181); Tickell fool-
ishly thinks Addison initialed his *Spectator* pieces to avoid "usurp-
ing the praise of others" (2:105); Fenton naively implies that only
Roscommon's severe judgment kept him from being prolific
(1:234–35).

In general, Johnson is especially wary of sources' favorable
biases, but he also notes when testimony is consistently hostile.
For example, he notes that "Burnet is not very favourable to his
[Sprat's] memory" because "he and Burnet were old rivals" (2:37).
Johnson recognizes that, to some extent, most testimony is potentially hostile; everyone envies the great, and thus everyone has
some interest in spreading unflattering stories: "By tales like these
is the envy raised by superior abilities every day gratified" (2:182).

Johnson's suspicions are also frequently aroused by internal
evidence that testimony is doubtful; in Locke's terms, either inter-

nal contradiction or unlikely circumstances may call a piece of testimony into doubt.

Johnson's frequent analyses of internal contradictions bring to mind the image of Johnson as a lawyer cross-examining witnesses. He cites Dryden's self-defense against the charge of plagiarism in one breath and in the next points out that Dryden nevertheless "relates how much labour he spends in fitting for the English stage what he borrows from others" (1:347–48). In the *Life of Butler*, Johnson cites Butler's brother as a witness that Butler attended Cambridge—but finds inconsistent his inability to identify his college, which "gives reason to suspect that he was resolved to bestow on him an academical education" (1:202).

Johnson's most characteristic doubts, however, are stirred up by improbable circumstances. In this area Johnson most clearly enjoys displaying his skepticism and showing the power of independent judgment operating upon experience. Rather than simply setting aside doubtful pieces of testimony, he exhibits them in good Baylean fashion and exposes their unlikeliness. Often the occasions for Johnson's doubts are relatively unimportant. He devotes a paragraph to probable arguments against the trivial though much discussed notion that Milton's daughter could recite the opening lines of Homer, Ovid, and Euripides (1:158–59). He argues against Swift's belief that eating fruit caused his ear malady: "Almost every boy eats as much fruit as he can get, without any great inconvenience" (3:4). He finds it unlikely that one of Pope's instructors "could spend, with a boy who had translated so much of *Ovid*, some months over a small part of Tully's *Offices*" (3:86). With some typically Johnsonian calculations he attacks the apparently grandiose claim that William King read and wrote comments on 22,000 books and manuscripts: "The books were certainly not long, the manuscripts not very difficult, nor the remarks very large; for the calculator will find that he dispatched seven a day, for every day of his eight years, with a remnant that more than satisfies most other students" (2:26).

Johnson has a keen eye for improbable behavior. As a student of the passions, Johnson knows the effects of envy too well to believe that John Philips "so much endeared himself to his schoolfellows . . . that they without murmur or ill-will saw him indulged by the master with particular immunities" (1:312). As a writer well acquainted with the rigors of authorship, Johnson doubts that Christopher Pitt translated Virgil "with great indifference, and with a progress of which himself was hardly conscious" (3:278). And as a careful observer of social behavior, Johnson doubts that Addison was as shy as Chesterfield claimed: "That man cannot be supposed very unexpert in the arts of conversation and practice of life, who, without fortune or alliance, by his usefulness and dexterity became secretary of state" (2:119). In such passages we feel Johnson's skepticism at its most forceful. His arguments based on his knowledge of probable human behavior are persuasive and final.

Examples of Johnson's doubts arising from Locke's final criterion, contrary testimony, have already been discussed by implication; Johnson evaluates contrary testimony whenever he collates and compares various biographical sources. He uses an interesting rule of thumb: a person's enemies give more credible testimony for him than his friends do. We know that Swift worked hard to promote Pope's subscriptions because "there remains the testimony of Kennet, no friend to either him or Pope" (3:130), and Blackmore, though "oftener mentioned by enemies than by friends," was never reproached for any failings in his private life (2:236, 254–55). The view of Addison given by his friends "was never contradicted by his enemies" (2:125) and may therefore be believed. Prior "lived at a time when the rage of party detected all which it was any man's interest to hide; and as little ill is heard of Prior it is certain that not much is known" (2:197).

Johnson, Skepticism, and
Biography

In the handling of biographical testimony, then, Johnson's practice fully accords with the Lockean criteria for evaluating the evidence of witnesses: collate and compare sources when evidence is scanty; weigh the witnesses' skill and integrity, particularly noting hostile and favorable biases and tendencies to flatter self or subject; weigh the witness's overall intentions; set aside evidence marred by unlikely circumstances or internal contradictions; resolve contradictions by giving added weight to such probable testimony as favorable accounts from hostile witnesses.

Johnson's importance as a founder of literary biography rests partly on his willingness to go still further in using literary evidence. Precisely because of his "skeptical attitude toward the biographical validity of literary statements," he provides splendid illustrations of how one may properly use an author's works as evidence of his character.[9] The best examples are his extended analyses of Dryden and Pope, which link the authors' personalities and works. In this area, as in others, Johnson sets a skeptical example for future literary biographers because he is vigorously aware of the dangers of drawing biographical inferences from literary works. And while the skeptical tone and method of Johnson's biographies owe much to the skeptical modes of argument in the religious, scientific, and philosophical writings of his day, Johnson's biographical skepticism is grounded finally in his awareness of the difficulty of inferentially knowing another human being. His skepticism, in fact, is subsumed by his irony; the wish to understand another human being sometimes becomes another vain human wish which life ironically frustrates. He recognizes the ironies of the biographer's effort, which is merely the human effort to understand another, to understand one another:

> The biographer of Thomson has remarked that an author's life is best read in his works: his observation was not well timed. Savage, who lived much with Thomson, once told me how he heard

The Philosophical
Biographer

a lady remarking that she could gather from his works three parts of his character, that he was "a great lover, a great swimmer, and rigorously abstinent"; but, said Savage, he knows not any love but that of the sex; he was perhaps never in cold water in his life; and he indulges himself in all the luxury that comes within his reach. [3:297–98]

Four

Satire and Sympathy

in the

Life of Savage

The *Life of Savage* is an acknowledged masterpiece of biography, yet it is usually praised in decidedly nonliterary terms. One reason for this misplaced emphasis is that biography itself, as A. O. J. Cockshut reminds us, is a neglected form (11–15). Since a biography deals with facts and the interpretation of facts, Cockshut notes, readers tend to assume that it can best be evaluated by its accuracy and insight (11). Ira Bruce Nadel stresses the same point: "Readers of biography consistently ignore . . . what is written in favour of what is written about, treating the narrative transparently" (3). Johnson's fairness and compassion, his ability to present all the evidence despite his friendship with Savage, his powers of psychological insight—all of these well-known virtues of Johnson's treatment of Savage pertain more to the author's role as an accurate observer than to his skill as a writer. Critics have tended to argue that Johnson has revealed Savage; they have been less ready to admit that Johnson has created him. They tend to

forget the artfulness of the biographer, whose rhetoric is complicated by his role as "both an interpreter and an object of interpretation" (Nadel 2).

This potential opposition of artistry and accuracy is inherent
in the genre of biography; the pressure of this opposition has been
felt since the rise of the novel as a dominant form, with novels
imitating lives and lives imitating novels. In the early eighteenth
century, an especially interesting process of cross-fertilization
took place, as biographical fictions by Defoe and others enriched
the novel's development even while they set dangerous (and chal-
lenging) precedents for future biographers. Donald Stauffer describes Defoe's influence this way: "He is the great master in the
art of telling a lie; this gift is no fit legacy for biographers. Almost
to the same extent that novels written in his school seem more
credible than earlier romances, so biographies written under his
influence arouse more doubt, skepticism or sheer bewilderment
as to their authenticity" (1:78). From Stauffer's remark it appears
that in biography a too evident narrative artistry can destroy the
very sense of authenticity it is meant to foster. Carry this idea a
step farther, and it may appear that the best way to seem authen-
tic is to seem artless—a lesson which Defoe successfully applied
to the writing of fiction. Perhaps literary critics tend to approach
Johnson's *Life of Savage* primarily as a historical and psychological document because of this potential opposition: praise Johnson's artistry, and you find that the life can no longer be treated as
a direct, relatively unfiltered expression of his insights.

As we read the biography, in fact, the intricacies of Johnson's
relationship with Savage constantly distract us from the merits of
Johnson's narrative techniques. Johnson knew his subject well; he
loved Savage but saw him clearly. Johnson's skill at drawing subtle moral distinctions was especially suited to the analysis of so
complex a mixture of virtues and failings as Savage, and Johnson's

Satire in the
Life of Savage

later emphasis (in his theoretical statements on biography) upon
the exemplary and didactic functions of biography might indicate
that even in this early life he had to treat the attractive but folly-
ridden hero with special care.[1] Given all of these circumstances,
how could the *Life of Savage* have been anything but vital and
engrossing?

Of course, few critics praise the life in such baldly extrinsic
terms, but it is common to praise Johnson-as-observer rather than
Johnson-as-writer in speaking of this work.[2] It seems a perfect
embodiment of Johnson's complexity and breadth of emotional
response; in it one sees him moving back and forth between ironic
and sympathetic attitudes, between pathos and ridicule, between
private friendship and the detached impartiality of the public biographer. These alternating impulses are expressed by Johnson the
writer; they are sensed by the reader and are attributed to Johnson the observer.

It is not surprising, therefore, that critics have seen in the *Life
of Savage* signs of conflicting emotions and intentions. Joseph
Wood Krutch claims that Johnson's "preposterous partiality" in
Savage's favor conflicts with his goal of biographical fairness;
Johnson's triumph is his refusal to withhold even potentially
damning evidence (82). James Clifford sees Johnson reconciling
contradictory intentions: "Throughout, Johnson was an objective
moralist as well as an impassioned partisan. The two often conflicting intentions gave the work its depth and balance." According to Clifford's account, the life "came as a happy accident from
the union of powerful emotion and deep curiosity about human
nature" (*Young Sam Johnson* 277). Even Clarence Tracy occasionally writes with surprising certainty about Johnson's inner conflicts: "He gave the facts [about Savage's writing a satire while in
prison] as objectively as he could, and then broke out with amaze-
ment: 'Such was his Impudence'" (*Life of Savage* xix).

Despite their attention to Johnson's thoughts and motivations, Krutch and Clifford have little to say about the literary excellence of the *Life of Savage*—its excellence as a carefully designed prose narrative, that is, rather than as a psychological document. Perhaps because they are mainly concerned with analyzing Johnson's inner responses, these critics implicitly regard the biography itself as the direct expression of Johnson's feelings; as a result they do not attend to the appearance of artistry or to the means the author employs to direct our feelings.

Among the exceptions to this tendency to praise Johnson's insight rather than his artistry are Paul Alkon, who applies reader-response theory to the *Life*, and William Vesterman, who attacks Krutch's theory of conflicting intentions and concludes that Johnson's style is shaped by his "resistance to the melodrama of his material": Johnson "refuses to assume the literary equivalent of the melodramatic 'benevolence' afforded to Savage in his life, a kind of sympathy which, as Johnson demonstrates, did him no lasting good. . . . Johnson's own explicit expressions of sympathy seldom go beyond calling Savage an 'unhappy man.' Yet the very rigor of his restraint measures the force of the love and sorrow it holds back" (*Stylistic Life* 28). According to this account, Johnson handles the opposition between personal sympathy and moral duty by rising above the conflict itself. Vesterman properly demonstrates how Johnson portrays Savage as the object of emotionally extreme responses; during his lifetime Savage was as much the victim of misplaced benevolence as of violent resentment, and it does seem that Johnson carefully avoids these extremes in his own treatment of Savage.

Nevertheless, like the other critics mentioned, Vesterman too easily assumes that the style unequivocally embodies Johnson's attitudes. He analyzes the biography primarily to reveal the fullness and complexity of the biographer's responses; he asserts too positively that "Johnson's real feelings about Savage are found everywhere in *The Life of Savage*" (*Stylistic Life* 40).

What concerns us is not whether Johnson's narrative techniques are sincere or calculated, conscious or unconscious, internalized or externalized; we want to know how they function to make the *Life of Savage* a great biography. As Nadel has noted, "when a biographer recognizes that the life he writes is itself an aesthetic construct involving fictions, imagery, style and narration, parallel to the inner life of its subject, itself a fiction, the result may be a biography that is at the same time literary and truthful. It will also reflect the ambiguous, self-contradictory, illogical individual that is its subject" (Nadel 118). We can hardly entertain the notion that Johnson's style transcends an underlying conflict of emotions without at least considering the possibility that a gifted author uses emotional conflict as a way of shaping the reader's attitudes toward Savage. If Johnson arouses expectations of moral condemnation but then reverses the field and produces reasons for compassion, the result is powerfully affective. Our impulse to respond harshly is checked and frustrated by a reaction. The qualities of balance and antithesis prevalent in Johnson's style are admirably suited to this particular kind of arousal and frustration of expectations. In the *Life of Savage* Johnson's complex biographical rhetoric may or may not express his doubts about his subject, but it certainly manipulates his reader's expectations.

Authorial intentions are difficult to prove, but audience expectations are less so. As Benjamin Boyce's source study clearly shows, by the time Johnson wrote the *Life of Savage*, a decades-long stream of publications had already turned its protagonist into a semimythological or folkloric figure. Johnson was writing for an audience already primed to see Savage's story in pathetic and melodramatic terms on the one hand or in ironic and satiric terms on the other. Whatever Johnson's own feelings—ambivalent or otherwise—Savage's story was fascinating to eighteenth-century readers partly because it embodied *society's* ambivalence about a wide range of issues: kinship, bonds of familial affection, patronage, social rank in relation to individual merit, and others. Stirred by the rich potentialities of his subject, Johnson happened upon what would remain a key feature of his biographical technique: he approached Savage as a problem in moral judgment, and he aimed for balance by setting up an alternating motion between sympathetic and objective poles of response, or as Paul Alkon more accurately describes it, a "complicated double motion of identification followed by avoidance" ("Intention and Reception" 142). Alkon observes that in this way Johnson achieved an early solution to a biographical dilemma: "a central problem that occupied novelists and biographers alike during the next two centuries . . . [was] to evolve narrative techniques that would allow an inside view of characters adequate to elicit reader identification, while at the same time maintaining sufficient ethical distance to ensure proper moral judgment" ("Intention and Reception" 145).

Paradoxically, when a writer uses dialectical shifts of perspective or of emotional response, we tend to describe such a style as judicious and restrained, forgetting that the impression of restraint results from the conflict of opposing forces: "That he did not execute this design [i.e., Savage's proposed *Progress of the Freethinker*] is a real loss to mankind, for he was too well acquainted with all the scenes of debauchery to have failed in his representations of them, and too zealous for virtue not to have represented them in such a manner as should expose them either to ridicule or detestation."[3] The first clause arouses expectations of genuine praise; the second clause ironically subverts this expectation; and the third clause surprisingly satisfies it. The final effect is one of absolute fairness, but the means by which that effect is achieved

Satire in the
Life of Savage

is the opposition of contrary impulses: toward satire on the one hand, and toward encomium on the other.

Johnson employs this pattern not only in the structure of individual sentences but also in the structure of the life as a whole. He arouses expectations of emotional release, then frustrates these expectations by bringing other emotions into play; he uses the same pattern of conflict in handling material from both ends of the spectrum of reader response. At one pole there is complete sympathetic identification with Savage; the emotions aroused are pity for Savage and anger against those who victimize him. At the other pole there is complete detachment from Savage; the emotions aroused are amusement at Savage's folly and satiric derision against his oppressors.[4]

Savage's life, in the various forms in which it was already familiar to the reading public of the 1740s, was a story richly laced with the elements of pathos. One reason for the popularity of life histories of disenfranchised noble bastards was that they allowed a plentiful indulgence in pathos and in sympathetic identification with the hero's sufferings at the hands of a vengeful parent. Boyce cites, for example, a life history nearly contemporaneous with the *Life of Savage:* the memoirs of James Annesley, published as *Memoirs of an Unfortunate Young Nobleman* and digested in the *Gentleman's Magazine*, February to June 1743 (see "Johnson's *Life of Savage*" 588–90).

In dealing with Savage's relations with his mother, Johnson could follow his sources, including Savage's own maudlin writings, which emphasized the pathos of Savage's helplessness and his mother's cruelty, and thereby risk making this entire part of the story seem less credible, or he could coolly recount the facts of the case (as he knew them) and let her malice speak for itself. The printed biographical sources Johnson had to work with used the former approach, sometimes to the point of being melodramatic. In a sense Johnson follows their lead, but he manages to

heighten our sense of Mrs. Brett's malice and Savage's helplessness without seeming to indulge in exaggeration or emotional
excess. His dialectical alternations of emotional response help
him solve a problem of plausibility: how to portray incredible evil
in a way that renders it credible. Seen in another way, these alternations help Johnson solve a problem in narrative technique: how
to maintain "accuracy of presentation" while telling the story
from the viewpoint of a dramatic narrator who is involved with
his subject (Nadel 172).

He begins, in paragraph 5, by setting out the facts (although
he had them wrong) in what Boyce calls "the rapid, dry manner,
seemingly utterly reliable, of the better criminal biographies"
("Johnson's *Life of Savage*" 591). Then, in the middle of paragraph
6, he begins the first of his analyses of the Countess's motives: "It is
not indeed easy to discover what motives could be found to over-
balance that natural affection of a parent, or what interest could be
promoted by neglect or cruelty" (2:323). This is what readers want
from an accurate biographer: confronted by improbability, he is
bound to seek motives and explanations. But under cover of inves-
tigating her motives, Johnson begins to introduce the kind of pathetic language one finds in the Annesley *Memoirs:*

> It was therefore not likely that she would be wicked without
> temptation, that she would look upon her son from his birth with
> a kind of resentment and abhorrence, and, instead of supporting,
> assisting, and defending him, delight to see him struggling with
> misery; or that she would take every opportunity of aggravating
> his misfortunes and obstructing his resources, and with an impla-
> cable and restless cruelty continue her persecution from the first
> hour of his life to the last. [2:323–24]

Here Johnson's syntax functions with great expressive power; we
seem to feel his anger forcing its way to the surface, gathering
momentum for a final denunciation. Characteristically, however,

the author frustrates this expectation of release by reverting to the dry style of paragraph 7: "But whatever were her motives." The manner may be intuitive, but it is artful and does its work. Johnson manages simultaneously to characterize the Countess vividly and to disarm the reader's potential incredulity by insisting that her behavior *was* astonishing.

In paragraph 8 Johnson interrupts the narrative flow for the first of his recapitulations. The retrospect functions not so much as a narrative summary (one hardly needs a summary at this early point in the life) as a shift in perspective, an invitation to step back and see Savage's situation in relation to past and future. Here, where the break in the narrative pulls us back from our absorption in the story, Johnson feels free to permit emotional release through the use of heightened figurative language: Savage was "doomed to poverty and obscurity, and launched upon the ocean of life only that he might be swallowed by its quicksands or dashed upon its rocks." It is as though Johnson's emotion has gathered force during the actual narrative, then overflows during the recapitulation:

> In this manner were passed those days and those nights which nature had enabled him to have employed in elevated speculations, useful studies, or pleasing conversation. On a bulk, in a cellar, or in a glass-house among thieves and beggars was to be found the Author of *The Wanderer*, the man of exalted sentiments, extensive views, and curious observations; the man whose remarks of life might have assisted the statesman, whose ideas of virtue might have enlightened the moralist, whose eloquence might have influenced senates, and whose delicacy might have polished courts. [2:399]

These recapitulations sharpen the pathos of Savage's case; but their vividly emphatic language also suggests the author's moral distress over this waste of great abilities. It is significant that John-

son introduces the emotionally colored language with simple, restrained pointing gestures: "Such was . . ." or "In this manner . . ." He pulls us away from our involvement in the story
with such gestures again and again (see 2:409 and 425 in particular). We seem to feel the author's emotion forcing its way into the
narrative, breaking its continuity, erupting into pathos—yet the
effect is anything but careless.

The credibility of the narrative in fact derives largely from the
compassionate but skeptical ethos of the narrative voice; the narrator enacts our skepticism for us and thus disarms us, enabling
us to sympathize. Because Johnson adopts the technique of nar-
rating the story "from the viewpoint of a wise, detached narrator
closely following and often describing the protagonist's mind, [it
was] . . . essential, or at least advantageous, to conceal Mrs.
Brett's motives by turning her, as Johnson does, into a frightening
figure whose actions remain wholly unaccountable in terms of
ordinary human psychology" (Alkon, "Intention and Reception"
148). When Mrs. Brett denies that Savage is alive in order to cut
him off from his rightful inheritance, Johnson remarks upon the
improbability of her behavior by commenting that this "is perhaps the first instance of a lie invented by a mother to deprive her
son of a provision which was designed him by another, and which
she could not expect herself, though he should lose it" (2:326–27).
To render her behavior thoroughly probable would require an
explanation of her motivation to account for the underlying
causes of which her actions are consequences or "signs," to use the
language of probability; but Johnson instead insists upon the absence of such explanations. The Countess's act is so "unnatural"
(in the sense of "contrary to normal laws of probable behavior")
that it gives her great tactical advantages: "the Earl did not imagine there could exist in human form a mother that would ruin her
son without enriching herself" (2:327). When she tries to have
Savage shipped off to the colonies, Johnson suggests that she

could not find accomplices wicked enough to help a woman who would harm her son "without interest, and without provocation" (2:327). Savage's pardon, "with whatever difficulty the story may obtain belief, was obstructed only by his mother" (2:351). Eventually Johnson discusses her lack of probable motives at great length and uses this opportunity to reintroduce the language of strong condemnation (2:353). It is not quite enough to say that Johnson "refuses to react to Savage's mother as if she were Cruelty in Human Form" (Vesterman, *Stylistic Life* 665). It is significant that Johnson repeatedly draws the reader's attention to this refusal yet subtly implies that she takes a satanic pleasure in evildoing.[5]

Thus the final effect of these passages, despite the harshness of Johnson's language, is partly one of restraint; Johnson is apparently almost ready to pronounce her a monster but is determined to find an explanation that would fit her into some pattern of probable behavior. Our tendency to object that Mrs. Brett behaves more like a villainess in romance than like a real woman is beautifully checked by Johnson's insistence that her behavior was incredible.

There may be an undercurrent of irony in Johnson's entire strategy of seeming to hunt for rational explanations for evil; after all, it was Soame Jenyns, a writer determined to explain evil as a part of the natural order, who years later provoked Johnson's most severe satire—his review of Jenyns's *A Free Inquiry into the Nature and Origin of Evil*. Johnson openly assumes, in the passages quoted, that readers expect evildoing to be explicable in terms of self-interest, but seen from a higher point of view than that of the public biographer, who is bound to seek plausible explanations, this assumption overlooks the comprehensive explanation of evil offered by Christian doctrine. Thus the ironic effect of these passages is almost that of a naive satiric persona, with two reservations: first, that motive hunting is sometimes pointless but is not an absurd activity for a biographer and, second, that the irony remains ambiguous.

If Johnson's search for explanations had been more than a way of controlling the reader's attitude toward a potentially improbable set of behaviors, there might have been room in it for a simple hypothesis that explains Mrs. Brett's actions in a single stroke: she knew or believed Savage to be an impostor and did everything she could to defeat him because she saw him as an extortionist. I cannot believe that this hypothesis never occurred to Johnson, but it is conspicuously absent from the *Life*.[6]

Johnson's control over the reader's sympathies involves a process of anticipating expectations, heightening them, and finally curbing them or allowing them only limited release. The reader will expect a probable explanation of Mrs. Brett's actions; Johnson heightens this expectation and then dissipates it or turns it in a new direction. When the reader objects that her behavior is unnatural, he hears Johnson stress its incredibility, thereby indirectly winning credit for his own veracity. The reader will expect harsh language directed against her evildoing, and a plentiful appeal to the emotions; Johnson introduces harsh, emotional diction as though forced to do so by the sheer inexplicability of unmotivated evil. Johnson achieves pathos through indirection.

Johnson's irony brings him close to the methods of the satirist, and the recurrent emergence and suppression of satiric impulses in the *Life of Savage* is part of what W. J. Bate sees as a pervasive tendency in Johnson's works: "Ridicule, anger, satiric protest, are always in the process of turning into something else" ("Johnson and Satire Manqué" 150). He cites as one example the passage from the *Life of Savage* in which Savage rationalizes the unpopularity of his works (having earlier used the popularity of *The Bastard* to prove his own worth):

> either they were published at a time when the town was empty,
> or when the attention of the publick was engrossed by some

struggle in the parliament, or some other object of general concern; or they were by the neglect of the publisher not diligently
dispersed, or by his avarice not advertised with sufficient frequency. Address, or industry, or liberality, was always wanting;
and the blame was laid rather on any person than the author.
[2:379]

Johnson immediately softens this ridicule by moving toward sympathetic identification, noting in the next paragraph that we all
use "arts like these" to palliate our sufferings. The emotional
thrust is redirected: first one sees Savage's folly exhibited, but
then one identifies with his suffering. Satire and sympathetic
viewpoints modify each other in Johnson's emotional dialectic.

As Donald Siebert observes, from Johnson's point of view
Savage was in many ways a sympathetic figure and thus not a
proper object of satiric attack:

It is well to remember just how many factors are working against
even the possibility of satire in the *Life*—or at least a satirical
treatment of Savage himself. On Johnson's terms, Savage was not
in many respects a proper object of satire. He had suffered
enough already, and Johnson makes this bar to satire explicit
when he says Savage himself learned "that distress was not a
proper subject for merriment, or topick of invective." ["Style of
Satire" 103]

But if Savage is not treated as a satiric butt, the rising and falling
curve of his personal fortune makes him the perfect spokesman
for satire directed outward against his acquaintances. As Savage's
reputation rises, we see his circle of friends widen and brighten;
amid this glitter, moving among the great but still an outsider,
Savage himself becomes a satirist:

As the reputation of his abilities . . . intitled him to familiarity
with persons of higher rank than those to whose conversation he

had been before admitted, he did not fail to gratify that curiosity
which induced him to take a nearer view of those whom their
birth, their employments, or their fortunes, necessarily place at a
distance from the greatest part of mankind, and to examine
whether their merit was magnified or diminished by the medium
through which it was contemplated; whether the splendour with
which they dazzled their admirers was inherent in themselves, or
only reflected on them by the objects that surrounded them; and
whether great men were selected for high stations, or high stations made great men. [2:370–71]

The result of Savage's researches, as Johnson notes in delicate
understatement, was that "he did not appear to have formed very
elevated ideas of those to whom the administration of affairs or
the conduct of parties has been entrusted" (2:372).

Johnson's Juvenalian irony gives the life a thematic coherence
it would otherwise have lacked. One of the great morals of the *Life
of Savage* is particularly Juvenalian: neither affluence nor power,
nor even extraordinary abilities, ever brought Savage any lasting
happiness. The two former qualities are "advantages extrinsick
and adventitious" (2:321), and one expects their effects to be tran-
sitory, but when people start judging Savage's abilities in terms of
his affluence and power (always a sensitive subject for Johnson),
we have a situation in which bitter satire is called for: "He com-
plained that as his affairs grew desperate he found his reputation
for capacity visibly decline, that his opinion in questions of criticism was no longer regarded when his coat was out of fashion"
(2:403). This reductive witticism is followed by a catalog of dis-
couragements condescendingly enumerated by Savage's friends,
and by letting Savage recount them in indirect discourse, Johnson
gently reminds us that Savage's satiric outburst stems from a just
sense of personal injury. What is more, the analogy between Sav-

age's criticism and his coat, as John Dussinger accurately observes, is part of a continuing satiric theme in the *Life:* recurrent references to Savage's clothes reduce him "to a thing to be dressed, an article to be measured and draped according to the wishes of those few acquaintances willing to pay the price" (*Discourse* 144). Of course, in this instance, the unsympathetic effect of the wit itself is softened by the fact that Johnson is indirectly quoting Savage's own words.

The point is that Johnson uses Savage often as a satiric spokesman but seldom as a satiric butt; in dealing with Savage he rarely establishes a sustained satiric tone. Instead, flashes of wit at Savage's expense occur at unexpected places in the life, and they contribute to our sense that the author is holding dangerous forces of ridicule tightly in check.

For example, after recounting the story of Savage's break with Lord Tyrconnel, Johnson epigrammatically sums up Savage: "It was his peculiar happiness that he scarcely ever found a stranger whom he did not leave a friend; but it must likewise be added that he had not often a friend long, without obliging him to become a stranger" (2:369). Again, after quoting a letter written by Savage from prison as evidence of the "cheerfulness with which he bore his confinement," Johnson comments:

> Surely the fortitude of this man deserves, at least, to be mentioned with applause; and, whatever faults may be imputed to him, the virtue of suffering well cannot be denied him. The two powers which, in the opinion of Epictetus, constituted a wise man are those of bearing and forbearing, which cannot indeed be affirmed to have been equally possessed by Savage; and indeed the want of one obliged him very frequently to practice the other. [2:423]

This last clause is satiric verbal wit in a concentrated form—taking an unexpected play on words and making it morally incisive.

The Philosophical
Biographer

In another spot, as he describes Savage's intellectual powers, Johnson strikes a witty sidelong blow at his inconsistency: "He was remarkably retentive of his ideas, which, when once he was in possession of them, rarely forsook him; a quality which could never be communicated to his money" (2:403). In each of these examples, the witticism is so placed that it appears to be an after-thought rather than a contrived effect. The reader can therefore enjoy the playfulness of the wit without feeling that it is unsympathetic or that the author has cruelly mocked Savage.

Similarly, in dealing with Savage, Johnson employs one ironic figure so subdued that it is seldom noticed. To describe a person's advantages, Johnson repeatedly uses a triple formula like that found in paragraph 2: "affluence," "power," and "intellectual greatness" (2:321). There are variants of the formula: "persons eminent for their rank, their virtue, and their wit" (2:341) or "those whom their birth, their employments, or their fortunes, necessarily place at a distance" (2:371). When speaking of Savage, Johnson plays against the expectations aroused by this formula: "He therefore exerted all the interest which his wit, or his birth, or his *mis*fortunes, could procure" (2:381; italics added). "Mr. Savage made no scruple of asserting that his birth, his *mis*fortunes, and his genius gave him a fairer title than could be pleaded by him on whom it [the laureateship] was conferred" (2:404; italics added). This sort of irony does not call attention to itself, but it does subtly remind us that Savage used his disadvantages to advance himself and that his misfortunes paradoxically made his fortune.

The final two paragraphs of the *Life of Savage* epitomize Johnson's method of curbing one impulse by bringing another into play. The story of Savage's life, Johnson seems to be saying, must inevitably stir contradictory emotions, but justice demands that we hold them all in balance. While Savage's case was unique, it was also representative: we all share some of his virtues and some of his vices. To make the reader share Johnson's humane and compassionate recognition of the mixture of wisdom and folly, vice and virtue, in every human soul—this is the final purpose of his balancing of impulses. His *Life of Savage* is a triumph not just because Johnson himself was moved by conflicting intentions and emotions toward Savage (although there is, as I have admitted, some truth in such a view), but because he found uniquely appropriate techniques to create a dynamic conflict of emotions within the reader. This vigorous dialectic of satire and sympathy in the *Life of Savage* anticipates the broader dialectical tendencies of Johnson's other biographies in the *Lives of the Poets*, written more than thirty years later.

Five

Johnson's Redaction of

Hawkesworth's

Swift

The skeptical redaction of source material is a biographical technique that Johnson perfected as early as the *Life of Savage*, in which his approach is characterized by "resistance to the melodrama of his material" (Vesterman, "Johnson and *The Life of Savage*" 674). In the *Life of Swift*, Johnson's dialectical resistance to a previous biographer gives the biography an emotional vigor like that of the *Life of Savage* but only at the cost of some rather odd distortions as well.

The *Life of Swift* has always been a problem for Johnsonians. With the possible exception of the *Life of Milton*, it is the most blatantly unfair of Johnson's biographies, and its unfairness clearly resulted at least partly from the prejudice against Swift that is amply documented by Boswell's collection of Johnson's sometimes "embarrassingly juvenile" remarks about Swift (Hilles, "Swift's Last Years" 370). However, as W. B. C. Watkins noted, "behind this lifelong prejudice of Johnson's lies a far more

interesting complexity of beliefs and personality than the comparatively obvious explanations of his bias in his lives of Milton
and Gray" (27). Whatever Johnson's antipathy may have been, it
was mixed with admiration; he used Swift extensively in compil-
ing illustrations for the *Dictionary*, he used to quote Swift frequently, and several of his early satires imitated Swift's. Perhaps
Johnson's aggressiveness toward Swift reflected what is now commonly called identification, complicated by hostility arising from
shared personal characteristics and circumstances.[1] Perhaps, to
Johnson, Swift represented a portion of himself that he rejected,
"restrain[ing] in himself those tendencies to which Swift gave free
rein" (Watkins 32). But whatever the origins of his complex attitude toward Swift, the nature and extent of Johnson's distortions in his *Life of Swift* make it hard to believe Wayne Warncke's
argument that little more than conscious moralistic intention was
at work. Johnson's usual sense of balanced judgment went dras-
tically awry in the writing of the *Life*.

Admittedly, many of his mistakes seem to result from his "excessive haste, carelessness, and . . . usual habit of trusting to
memory" (Korshin, "Johnson and Swift" 466). Even the best-
known anecdote in the *Life of Swift*—"Cousin Swift, you will
never be a poet"—is a fiction based on a distortion "perfected" by
Johnson's misremembering (Maurice Johnson 1034). Sometimes
Johnson innocently repeats others' mistakes, as when he says,
perpetuating an error started by William Wotton (in his *Observations upon the "Tale of a Tub"* [1705]) that the *Battle of the Books* was
based upon a book called *Combat des livres*. But many of his "mistakes" are more blatantly and aggressively unfair, such as his
treatment of the question of Swift's birthplace, which, Johnson
says, should "be left in the obscurity in which he [Swift] de-
lighted to involve it" (3:2). Johnson makes this comment even
though the sources he used state unequivocally that Swift was

born in Dublin; Hawkesworth says this, as does Swift himself in his autobiographical fragment (published with Deane Swift's *Essay upon the Life, Writings, and Character, of Dr. Jonathan Swift* [London, 1755] and hence available to Johnson). "Is it not a little odd," Harold Williams wonders, "that Johnson should profess ignorance about a fact which was not in doubt, and which he had no real reason to pretend *was*?" (123). The small germ of truth upon which Johnson based his comment was the undeniable but trivial fact that Swift did like to think and speak of himself as an Englishman. But Johnson commits worse distortions than this one.

Speaking of Swift's self-proclaimed disinterestedness in serving the Tory ministry, Johnson comments, first, that such an attitude "would have been in his condition romantick and superfluous." Then, to show that Swift was in any case not as free from self-interest as he liked to claim, Johnson writes: "He refused, indeed, fifty pounds from Lord Oxford, but he accepted afterwards a draught of a thousand upon the Exchequer, which was intercepted by the Queen's death, and which he resigned, as he says himself, '*multa gemens*' (with many a groan)" (3:22–23). Here Johnson unfairly juxtaposes two incidents. Swift refused the first offer for perfectly understandable reasons: he felt that a gift of fifty pounds from Oxford, a personal friend, would have put him "on a level with hired party scribblers" (Williams 126). On the other hand, the one thousand pounds in question was meant to defray the costs of Swift's installation in the deanery of St. Patrick's. Thirteen years later Swift wrote jokingly to Pope: "I forgave Sir R—— W—— a thousand pounds, *multa gemens*" (*Correspondence* 3:159). Johnson manipulated his material by using selected instances and quotation out of context to suggest that Swift had his price.

There is also the episode of a letter to Queen Anne, written on behalf of a Mrs. Barber, the wife of a Dublin woollen draper. The letter was a grotesque counterfeit in an unidentified hand, with a big, clumsily forged signature. It bore only the crudest resemblance to Swift's style, and far from equivocating about its authorship, far from shuffling "between cowardice and veracity" (3:39), Swift immediately and effectively denied having had anything to do with it. His letters to Pope and to the Countess of Suffolk were unequivocal.

Lesser examples of Johnson's errors and distortions could be cited, but I have said enough to suggest that Johnson's accuracy and good biographical judgment were compromised in the writing of the *Life of Swift*. I believe that the reasons can be partly explained by looking at the influence upon Johnson of John Hawkesworth's *An Account of the Life of the Reverend Jonathan Swift*, first published in 1755 (to which I will hereafter refer simply as Hawkesworth's *Swift*). Johnson seems to have followed Hawkesworth closely, indeed often paragraph by paragraph, in writing his own biography of Swift.[2] I suspect that Johnson experienced a sort of double anxiety of influence—doubt about how to treat both his subject and his chief source—and that the *Life of Swift* is the problematic result. The relationship of Johnson's biography to Hawkesworth's prior account is close and complex, but comparison will show that Johnson's assertive personality leads him to rework Hawkesworth's text by resisting it, as though he were involved in a competitive dialogue with his departed friend.

Johnson's *Swift* begins, like many of the other *Lives*, with an acknowledgment of sources, but this acknowledgment is especially personal: "An Account of Dr. Swift has been already collected, with great diligence and acuteness, by Dr. Hawkesworth, according to a scheme which I laid before him in the intimacy of our friendship" (3:1). The acknowledgment is tantalizingly general, and one must join F. W. Hilles in wondering, "What were his 'thoughts'? What was that 'scheme'?" (Hilles, "Swift's Last Years" 375). Did Johnson recommend a particular way of proceeding? Did he make specific recommendations about form, sources, or documentation?

Even a dating of the "scheme" must remain speculative. Hawkesworth's modern biographer believes that the exact date of his acquaintance with Johnson is "probably forever obscured."[3] Since Johnson began to work for Cave at the *Gentleman's Magazine* in early 1738, and Hawkesworth signed on in 1740, we can only guess that a likely terminus a quo for their friendship is 1740. The friendship between the two men flourished during the 1740s, and during the 1750s Hawkesworth "lived," as Boswell phrased it, "in great intimacy with" Johnson (Boswell 1:234). Certainly the friendship was firm in 1752, when Hawkesworth sought Johnson's help with *The Adventurer*, and it went back as far as 1748, the year Johnson founded the Ivy Lane club, to which Hawkesworth belonged (Boswell 1:190).

Boswell records a remark that may shed light on the nature of Johnson's "scheme": "He praised Delaney's [*sic*] 'Observations on Swift'; said that his book and Lord Orrery's might both be true, though one viewed Swift more, and the other less favourably; and that, between both, we might have a complete notion of Swift" (3:249).

The notion of a dialectical comparison of sources is typical of Johnson's skeptical approach to biography, and I think Robert Folkenflik is right in guessing that Johnson's "scheme" was the use of Orrery and Delany as complementary sources (*Samuel Johnson, Biographer* 22). In addition to the collation and comparison of Lord Orrery's *Remarks on the Life and Writings of Dr. Swift* (1751) and Patrick Delany's *Observations upon Lord Orrery's Remarks* (1754), Johnson might have suggested other, more specific features of Hawkesworth's *Swift*—such as its rather scholarly inclusion of marginal annotations indicating the source of individual anecdotes, a fairly unusual practice in an eighteenth-century biography.

Johnson and Hawkesworth's
Swift

This comparison and conflation of sources must have looked even more practicable in 1755, when Deane Swift published his *Essay upon the Life . . . of Dr. Swift*, making possible the synthesis of three widely divergent views. Whatever Johnson's "scheme" entailed, its result was Hawkesworth's *Swift*, based on the three sources just mentioned, plus Swift's brief, fragmentary *Autobiography* and portions of his correspondence. In comparing these, Hawkesworth in effect laid Johnson's groundwork for him, and he approached the task with a good sense of the limitations of each source.

John Boyle, Lord Orrery, was a celebrity hunter who wrote his *Remarks* with the same self-aggrandizing motives that led him to seek out Swift's acquaintance in the first place. He would be pleased to see that he is still often described as "an intimate friend of Swift."[4] In fact he was in his mid-twenties when he sought out Swift, who was then sixty-three, "with but a short period in command of his faculties remaining to him" (Williams 115). Orrery's *Remarks* presented an uncomplimentary portrait of Swift, encumbered by unnecessary digressions and distorted by exhibitionistic self-display. Though it was attacked a number of times—by Delany, for instance, and by the learned scholar-printer William Bowyer, who wrote a satiric piece to argue ironically that Orrery could not possibly have written so bad a book as the *Remarks*—Orrery's compilation was pretty highly regarded in its day (Bowyer 432–49). To be fair, it gives a good account of Swift's political career and writings. It was one of Hawkesworth's main sources.

Dr. Patrick Delany's *Observations upon Lord Orrery's Remarks* (1754) was published anonymously. Delany was a friend of Swift, and his reply to Orrery is sympathetic to Swift; it contains the best character sketch of Swift in these early sources. But the general tone is nevertheless deferential to Orrery, and the *Observations* presents less information about Swift than Delany's opportunities lead us to hope for.

The Philosophical
Biographer

Deane Swift's *An Essay upon the Life, Writings, and Character, of Dr. Jonathan Swift* (1755) was written by Swift's "parson cousin" —a man who had some contact with Swift early in Swift's life but whose close acquaintance was even later than Orrery's. He had the advantage of some manuscripts, including thirty-nine letters of what was later called the *Journal to Stella*. His essay presented the most detailed view of Swift available, though he made errors in dates, facts, and annotations.

Hawkesworth's *Swift* synthesized these three accounts and Swift's autobiographical fragment, indicating sources by means of marginal citations. One can form a sense of Hawkesworth's relative use of his sources by noting that more than fifty citations refer to Deane Swift's *Essay*, thirty to Delany's *Observations*, thirteen to Orrery's *Remarks*, and several to miscellaneous sources, including Swift's autobiography and his letters.[5] Of the three secondary sources, only Deane Swift's makes an attempt to present a chronological account of Swift's life, though it wanders off and digresses. For the chronology, then, his account probably served as Hawkesworth's central source, with material from other sources introduced where appropriate. This point cannot be conclusively demonstrated, but I suspect that Hawkesworth used this method and that Johnson used it in turn, basing his own work on Hawkesworth.

Clearly the tripartite relationship between Johnson's *Life of Swift*, its subject, and its sources is peculiar and complex. Johnson was in effect revising a biography written by a close friend who had worked along lines Johnson himself had suggested—and this was a friend, moreover, whom Boswell was not alone in seeing as Johnson's "closest imitator" (1:252). Johnson was in fact dealing with not just one alter ego but two, and if Watkins is right in claiming that Johnson recognized his own prejudice and tried to compensate for it, then the *Life of Swift* should be recognized as one of the most curiously divided works in the Johnson canon (Watkins 28). In his resistance to Hawkesworth, Johnson achieves several of his finest effects, and his biographical artistry shows clearly when we compare his work to his predecessor's. Although it is not my primary intention to join the rescuers of the *Life of Swift*, a comparison will reveal something of Johnson's artfulness as well as his ambivalent treatment of his source material.

Before analyzing Johnson's indebtedness and resistance to Hawkesworth, one must consider another complication: Hawkesworth's prior indebtedness to Johnson. Again one must speculate, but it is likely that Hawkesworth knew at least the main outlines of Johnson's views on biography as a genre. By 1755, when Hawkesworth was composing his biography of Swift, Johnson had already exerted a general influence through his practice as a biographer and through such critical statements as *Rambler* 60 (1750), which stresses the importance of our identification with the subject of a biography, our interest in personal rather than public life, and our hunger for those anecdotal details "which give excellence to biography" (*Rambler* 60; Yale *Works* 3:323). Johnson's other great critical statement on biography, *Idler* 84, was published after Hawkesworth's *Swift*, but in conversation Johnson would surely have discussed some of the values he would later attribute to biography in his famous essay: the moral value of biography and the critical value of the biographer's attempts to "fortify veracity" by telling the truth about his subject (Yale *Works* 2:263).

Hawkesworth would certainly have known Johnson's early biographical masterpiece the *Life of Savage*, and in his own work he seems to try to imitate some of its effects. The closing paragraph of *Savage* may be placed alongside the closing paragraph of Hawkesworth's *Swift* to illustrate the point. Both biographies deal with subjects who were puzzling, even paradoxical mixtures of qualities that defied simplistic judgment. Furthermore, both men's lives were mythic, already shaped to some extent by communal memory, supplying the moralist with a ready and recognized example. First Johnson, mixing what Boswell called "bark and steel for the mind" (1:215), consolation and bitter truth:

> This relation will not be wholly without its use if those who languish under any part of his sufferings shall be enabled to fortify their patience by reflecting that they feel only those afflictions from which the abilities of Savage did not exempt him; or those who, in confidence of superior capacities or attainments, disregard the common maxims of life, shall be reminded that negligence and irregularity long continued will make knowledge useless, wit ridiculous, and genius contemptible. [2:434]

Now Hawkesworth on Swift:

> Such was Dr. *Jonathan Swift*, whose writings either stimulate mankind to sustain their dignity as rational and moral beings, by shewing how low they stand in mere animal nature, or fright them from indecency by holding up its picture before them in its native deformity: and whose life, with all the advantages of genius and learning, was a scale of infelicity gradually ascending till pain and anguish destroyed the faculties by which they were felt; while he was viewed at a distance with envy, he became a burden to himself; he was forsaken by his friends, and his memory has been loaded with unmerited reproach: his life therefore does not afford less instruction than his writings, since to the wise it may teach humility, and to the simple content. [75-76]

This is effectively, perhaps exaggeratedly Johnsonian in its attempt to sound the note of balanced appraisal. Hawkesworth's coupling and uncoupling syntax and his bisociative, paradoxical contrasts (great suffering despite great gifts, terrible isolation despite worldwide fame, an end of life more frightening than the writer's most shocking satires) create a mixture of sympathy and detachment similar to Johnson's in the *Life of Savage*.

On the other hand, Hawkesworth is thoroughly un-Johnsonian in several ways, the most important being his almost total avoidance of Swift's writings in his life of Swift, which is not a literary biography at all. In fact, Hawkesworth stresses Swift's clerical obligations throughout the life, but he scarcely mentions Swift's works. In literary criticism Hawkesworth's *Swift* supplied no precedents for Johnson.

Hawkesworth falls disappointingly short of the Johnsonian model in his rather too unskeptical admiration for Swift. Perhaps he does not consciously try to "hide the man," but he does "produce a hero," especially in his repeated mentions of Swift's associations with the great public figures of his day (*Idler* 84; Yale *Works* 2:262).

Also un-Johnsonian is Hawkesworth's prose style at its weakest. Occasionally his ear is of very poor tin indeed, deaf to even the most jarring alliteration: "From this time the doctor supported the interest of his new friends with all his power, in pamphlets, poems, and periodical papers" (19).

Hawkesworth is also sometimes unsuccessful in his attempts to moralize in the Johnsonian manner. He seldom intrudes to draw moral judgments from the story of Swift's life, but when he does so, the moralizing is indeed intrusive; he lacks Johnson's knack for making the moral seem to rise directly from the story. After praising Swift for the conscientious performance of his ecclesiastical duties, for instance, Hawkesworth wants to show that Swift's domestic worship was equally sincere, so he singles out Swift's earnest manner of saying grace: "That transient Act of adoration . . . which generally consists only in a mutter and a bow," we are told, was performed by Swift with "emphasis and fervor" (15). Then Hawkesworth comments in a stage whisper: "It is hoped that those who can no otherwise [*sic*] emulate the character of *Swift*, will attempt it in this act of religious decorum, and no longer affect either to be wits or fine gentlemen by a conduct directly contrary to so great an example" (15–16). The schoolmarmish tone of direct address makes one glad that Hawkesworth is generally more distant.

At times Hawkesworth's sheer prolixity makes the moralizing sound hollow and stilted, as in his comment on Swift's constant handouts to Dublin tradeswomen:

> His bounty had not indeed the indiscriminating ardour of blind instinct, and, if it had, it would not have been the instrument of equal happiness: to feed idleness is to propagate misery, and discourage virtue; but to insure the reward of industry is to bestow a benefit at once upon the individual and the public; it is to preserve from despair those who struggle with difficulty and disappointment, it is to supply food and rest to that labour which alone can make food tasteful and rest sweet, and to invigorate the community by the full use of those members which would otherwise become not only useless but hurtful, as a limb in which vital fluid ceases to circulate will not only wither but corrupt. [67]

In showing that it is better to help laborers than beggars, Hawkesworth strives mightily to achieve Johnsonian grandeur, but the terminal image of a corrupted limb is a distressing anticlimax.

At another point, one can see Hawkesworth's best and worst qualities as he draws a Johnsonian moral. He is considering Swift's letters to Stella, noting that we often experience self-satisfaction only through the vicarious satisfaction of those dear to us: "Whatever excellence we possess, or whatever honours we obtain, the pleasure which they produce is all relative to some particular favourite with whom we are tenderly connected, either by friendship or by love; or at most it terminates, like rays collected by a burning-glass, in a very small circle which is scarce more than a point, and like light becomes sensible only by reflection" (20).

Stripped of its overelaborateness, this is an interesting observation, appropriate to the letters later known as the *Journal to Stella*, but the expression is somewhat diffuse. The "or's" link and unlink confusingly, and the sentence ends with a mild anticlimax. The image of a burning glass (a nicely Johnsonian image at that, in its allusion to a phenomenon of natural science) places our attention on the focusing and concentration of light—that is precisely the point of the metaphor. But the addition of "reflection," although ingenious and functional in the way it extends the visual "ground" of the metaphor, is nevertheless finally just an afterthought that weakens the initial effect, shifting the comparison from the notion of concentration to the notion of reflection.

Whatever its weaknesses, Hawkesworth's *Swift* is a competent piece of work, and Johnson evidently respected it enough to use it as the framework for his own *Life of Swift*. Of course, some similarities between the two works may result from parallel borrowings from earlier sources—Orrery, Delany, and Deane Swift—and in fact Warncke's analysis of Johnson's sources argues that Johnson's biography is modeled after Orrery's. I disagree; as Paul Korshin has observed, Johnson's indebtedness to Hawkesworth is strikingly apparent in the ordering of the narrative ("Johnson and Swift" 469). In fact the two biographies can be read as parallel texts.

In scores of instances Johnson only lightly retouches Hawkesworth's phrasing. For instance, "he took a journey to *Leicester* that he might consult with his mother about what course of life to pursue" (Hawkesworth 7) becomes "he went to consult his mother, who then lived at Leicester, about the future course of his

life" (*Lives* 3:3). Similarly, "Sir *William* received him with great
kindness" (Hawkesworth 8) becomes "Temple received with sufficient kindness the nephew of his father's friend" (*Lives* 3:3). The
closest parallels occur in straightforward narrative accounts—of,
for example, Swift's preferments or his travels—and one could
argue that such parallelism is inevitable and perhaps merely coinci-
dental in a chronological narrative. But the similarities go beyond
coincidence:

> This disappointment was soon after followed by another; it hap-
> pened that the deanery of *Derry* became vacant, and it was the
> earl of *Berkeley*'s turn to dispose of it; yet . . . the secretary having
> received a bribe, the deanery was given to another upon pretence
> that *Swift* who was then more than thirty years old was too
> young, and he received instead the two livings of *Laracor* and
> *Rathbeggin* in the diocese of *Meath*, which together did not amount
> to half the value of the deanery. [Hawkesworth 14]

Compare Johnson:

> But he had more yet to suffer. Lord Berkeley had the disposal of
> the deanery of Derry, and Swift expected to obtain it, but by the
> secretary's influence, supposed to have been secured by a bribe, it
> was bestowed on somebody else; and Swift was dismissed with
> the livings of Laracor and Rathbeggin in the diocese of Meath,
> which together did not equal half the value of the deanery. [3:8–9]

Further evidence of Johnson's indebtedness to Hawkesworth may
be found in the corresponding treatments, not only of chronological sequences, but also of topics which could have been introduced at other points in the narrative. For instance, Johnson
follows Hawkesworth in discussing Swift's relationships with
Vanessa and Stella immediately after each one's death, although
these discussions could have been introduced elsewhere.

Additional evidence of Johnson's primary reliance on Hawkesworth is his similar treatment of prior sources. For instance,
Hawkesworth was struck by a divergence between Delany, who
said Swift was well received in Ireland in 1714, and Orrery and
Deane Swift, who said he was reviled. Hawkesworth suggests, in
passing, that the different receptions might have occurred at different times: Swift was associated with the ministry in power
"when he went to take possession [of his deanery]; but when he
returned to his deanery, the power of the tories and the dean's
credit at court were at an end" (31). Johnson borrows this hint:
"When Delany says that he was received with respect, he means
for the first fortnight, when he came to take legal possession; and
when Lord Orrery tells that he was pelted by the populace, he is
to be understood of the time when, after the Queen's death, he
became a settled resident" (3:26–27).

On the other hand, while Johnson borrows freely, and while
the overall coherence of Hawkesworth's *Swift* supplies his framework, he is far from limiting himself to a mere recapitulation or
refutation. He gives us fresh analysis of Swift's behavior and idio-
syncrasies. He also adds the publication history of Swift's works,
anecdotes from Spence, information from people who had known
Swift, and criticism of Swift's works.

There is in addition a consistent pattern of resistance in Johnson's reshaping of Hawkesworth's material, and an analysis of this
pattern reveals something about Johnson's biographical methods.
For example, it is sometimes assumed that Johnson set out to pillory Swift and that he used whatever rhetorical weapons were at
his disposal. On the contrary, an examination of Hawkesworth
shows that Johnson omits crucial and damaging anecdotal material that he could have used to portray Swift even more unsym-
pathetically than he did.

While Johnson's approach to Hawkesworth is marked by a
constant resistance, this is less a predictable pattern of rhetorical

The Philosophical
Biographer

opposition than a subtle shift in controlling attitude. Johnson resists all encomiastic tendencies, for one thing, but this resistance
is part of something larger: Johnson's whole approach is ironic in a
broad sense. He sees comedy and irony where Hawkesworth sees
none, and this tendency enables him to condense and give ironic
point to anecdotes which Hawkesworth treats diffusely and less
effectively.

Early in the chronology there is a small but revealing instance
in which Johnson's sense of humor leads him to see comedy that
Hawkesworth misses. Ever impressed by Swift's associations
with the great, Hawkesworth says that King William "admitted
him [Swift] to such familiarity that he . . . once offered to make
him a captain of horse" (8). Johnson rephrases the anecdote and
uses it not to show Swift's familiarity with royalty but to reveal
royal character: "King William's notions were all military, and he
expressed his kindness to Swift by offering to make him a captain
of horse" (3:3). In a small stroke of comedy achieved with tone
and cadence, Johnson highlights King William's myopic pre-
occupation with things military, adding to our enjoyment of the
amusingly inappropriate notion of Jonathan Swift as a cavalry
officer.

Occasionally one can spot Johnson in the act of seizing a hint
in Hawkesworth's *Swift* and drawing ironic implications from it.
In the following anecdote, what Johnson singles out from
Hawkesworth is the image of Swift receiving the Irish weavers,
dispensing advice to the tradesmen, and reigning over the populace in pseudomonarchical state; Johnson will condense Hawkesworth's tame and unfocused version in a couple of terse, sarcastic
phrases, far more tendentious and unfair but also more effective
than the original. First Hawkesworth:

> From this time [i.e., after the *Drapier's Letters*] the Dean's influence
> in Ireland was almost without bounds, he was consulted in what-

ever related to domestic policy, and in particular to trade. The
weavers always considered him as their patron and legislator,
after his proposal for the use of *Irish* manufactures, and came
frequently in a body to receive his advice in settling the rates of
their stuffs, and the wages of their journeymen; and when elec-
tions were depending for the city of *Dublin*, many corporations
refused to declare themselves, till they knew his sentiments and
inclinations. Over the populace he was the most absolute monarch that ever governed men, and he was regarded by persons of
every rank with veneration and esteem. [44–45]

Now Johnson's condensation:

He was from this important year the *oracle of the traders*, and the
idol of the rabble, and by consequence was feared and courted by
all to whom the kindness of the traders or the populace were
necessary. [3:36; italics added]

Johnson's sense of irony is awakened by praise; virtually any
sort of admiring words stirs his skeptical resistance. Hawkesworth's hyperbolic tendencies constantly elicit this response.
Johnson condenses and gives ironic point to certain elements of
Hawkesworth's extravagant praise of Stella, for instance:

Beauty, which alone has been the object of universal admiration
and desire, which alone has elevated the possessor from the lowest
to the highest station, has given dominion to folly, and armed
caprice with the power of life and death, was in *Stella* only the
ornament of intellectual greatness; and wit, which has rendered
deformity lovely, and conferred honour upon vice, was in her only
the decoration of such virtue, as without either wit or beauty
would have compelled affection, esteem, and reverence. [48]

From this rather blowsy Hawkesworthese, Johnson picks up
the doublet pattern ("Beauty . . . and wit" becomes "Beauty and

the power of pleasing"), but he reacts against the tone, turning it in the direction of irony and pathos, so that Stella's praiseworthy qualities only aggravate her misfortune: "Beauty and the power of pleasing, the greatest external advantages that woman can desire or possess, were fatal to the unfortunate Stella" (3:40–41).

There is a constant condensing tendency in Johnson's treatment of Hawkesworth, as though Hawkesworth's striving to sound like the author of the *Rambler* freed Johnson to be more abrupt by way of contrast. Hawkesworth sounds *Rambler*-like in his casuistical treatment of Swift's frugality, for instance: "If his oeconomy degenerated into avarice, it must be confessed that his avarice did not contract his bounty, and he suffers no degradation in his moral character, who, when the practice of any virtue is becoming more difficult, is yet able to exert it in the same degree" (68). Johnson reduces this to a simple matter of choice: "He only liked one mode of expence better than another, and saved merely that he might have something to give" (3:57).

If Johnson often seems to be replying to Hawkesworth, sometimes his habit "of catching a term dropped . . . by someone and . . . altering its implications" leads him to take an unintentional hint from Hawkesworth and to extract negative implications where Hawkesworth intended positive ones (Reichard 226). Hawkesworth aims to make Swift's return to St. Patrick's sound dramatic; he describes Swift as surviving complex political intrigues through sheer force of personal integrity:

> The archbishop of *Dublin* and some of his old friends in the chapter set themselves against his measures with all their force, and laboured to disappoint him in the exercise of his power by every sort of opposition and delay. But whatever prejudice they had conceived against him was soon removed, by the disinterested integrity of his conduct, which was so apparent and striking, that

they soon regarded him with respect and veneration, and almost
implicitly acquiesced in whatever he proposed. [32]

Hawkesworth's weighty, generalized diction and his dignified ca-
dences make this conflict sound important and intricate; Johnson's
language turns it into a minor squabble: "The Archbishop of Dublin gave him at first some disturbance in the exercise of his juris-
diction; but it was soon discovered, that between prudence and
integrity he was seldom in the wrong; and that, when he was
right, his spirit did not easily yield to opposition" (3:27). Johnson
draws from Hawkesworth the notion of integrity, but he insinu-
ates a judgment of Swift's motives by using the doublet "prudence and integrity" to imply that Swift acted sometimes from
merely prudential motives. Johnson removes the sense of total
victory implied by "respect and veneration," and he removes any
suggestion of Swift's disinterestedness, emphasizing instead his
refusal to yield.

Sometimes an added word or phrase gives Johnson's version a
startling, hostile tone. Nothing could be more opposite in effect
than Hawkesworth's and Johnson's comments on Stella's death,
for instance. Hawkesworth writes that Stella died "regretted by
the dean with such excess of affection and esteem as the keenest
sensibility only could feel, and the most excellent character ex-
cite" (48). Johnson's comment on Swift's love for Stella adds a
particularly damning phrase: "How much he wished her life his
papers show; nor can it be doubted that he dreaded the death of
her whom he loved most, *aggravated by the consciousness that himself
had hastened it*" (3:40; italics added).

It is not merely that Johnson tends to be censorious when
Hawkesworth is sympathetic—though that statement comes
close to the truth. Rather, Johnson seems to regard Hawkesworth
as somewhat naive and is constantly on guard against this naiveté.

There is a noticeable divergence of emphasis, for instance, when we reach the beginning of Swift's political involvement. Hawkesworth stresses Swift's intimacy with the great; the earlier biographer is too obviously a stargazer. In contrast, Johnson emphasizes the actual political conflict between Whigs and Tories. Thus Hawkesworth treats the *Conduct of the Allies* primarily as an example of Swift's celebrity and influence: "The tory members in both houses who spoke, drew all their arguments from it, and the resolutions which were printed in the votes, and which would never have passed but for the *Conduct of the Allies*, were little more than quotations from it" (22). Johnson shifts the emphasis outward to the general political situation, which diminishes the apparent importance of the tract, reducing the magnitude of Swift's influence by showing that it was a matter of accidental circumstances:

> The power of a political treatise depends much upon the disposition of the people: the nation was then combustible, and a spark set it on fire. . . . To [the tract's] propagation certainly no agency of power or influence was wanting. It furnished arguments for conversation, speeches for debate, and materials for parliamentary resolutions.
>
> Yet, surely, whoever surveys this wonder-working pamphlet with cool perusal will confess that its efficacy was supplied by the passions of its readers; that it operates by the mere weight of facts, with very little assistance from the hand that produced them.[6]

Johnson goes on to discuss Swift's familiarity with the great, but perhaps in resistance to Hawkesworth's celebrity worship, Johnson reduces Swift by performing a sort of reversal of figure and ground, suggesting that an affected attitude of familiarity is really a form of servility: Swift paid a "servile tribute to the Great . . . by suffering his liberty in their presence to aggrandize him in his own esteem" (3:21). As though pleased with the effect,

Johnson forces the reduction even further: "A servant eminently skilful may be saucy; but he is saucy only because he is servile" (3:22).

If Hawkesworth is overly impressed by Swift's familiar behavior with the highly placed, it is partly because he sees it, and wishes to use it, as a sign of Swift's integrity and disinterestedness. He even lumps them together syntactically at one point, saying that one of Swift's familiar jests "shews both his integrity and the freedom of his conversation with those who have a prescriptive right to servility and adulation" (21). Hawkesworth sounds particularly naive in asserting as "true" and "evident" Swift's claim that he did not expect to gain anything from his association with the Tory ministers (21). One would expect some awareness that a proud man like Swift might tend to protest too much in claiming independence and disavowing obligation to his political sponsors. Hawkesworth does admit that, since he is drawing most of the particulars concerning Swift's equality of behavior from the *Journal to Stella*, Swift may "be suspected of having somewhat exaggerated to gratify his vanity" (26), but then he quotes a letter to Oxford to prove that Swift was as independent as he claimed. He also overlooks, or at least fails to comment on, his own contradictory reference (on the very next page) to the St. Patrick's appointment as a reward procured for Swift by his friends and as something rather less than the bishopric one might have expected them to obtain for him.

Johnson subjects the question of Swift's preferment to brief but withering scrutiny. As we have seen, he regards Swift's imputed disinterestedness as "romantick and superfluous," for Swift had a right to expect some reward for his efforts, and he received one, in the form of his appointment to St. Patrick's (3:22).

Perhaps the single aspect of Hawkesworth's *Swift* that Johnson resists most vigorously is Hawkesworth's emphasis upon Swift's devotion to his clerical calling. Hawkesworth gives us the life of a clergyman who happened to be also a writer, while Johnson gives us the life of a writer who happened to be a clergyman. Hawkesworth admires Swift's devotion to his clerical duties, and Johnson, too, pays fair tribute to Swift's conscientiousness (Hawkesworth's *Swift* 15; *Lives* 3:53). But unlike Hawkesworth, Johnson has a demanding sense of the sort of behavior that is or is not suitable for a clergyman, and in his view, Swift seems to have fallen far short. Hawkesworth's incessant stress on Swift's devoutness generated powerful opposition from Johnson, who felt that Swift was a dangerous example of behavior inappropriate to a clergyman.

The reader expecting a literary biography will find it odd that Hawkesworth treats the beginning of Swift's life as a political writer in an offhand manner, making Swift sound like a preacher regretting his obligation toward a second, unsought political career. At several points in the biography, he makes it clear that he regards being a good preacher as the highest ambition Swift ever conceived: "He found it impracticable to excel as a preacher, his first and most laudable ambition" (35). Furthermore, Hawkesworth consistently portrays Swift as a clergyman who embodied the highest principles of Christian morality: his frugality was tempered by his charity, Hawkesworth says, while his seeming lack of tender, sympathetic impulses merely "transferred the distribution of his liberality from instinct to religion, and made that, which in others is an exercise of self-love, in him an act of obedience to God" (75). Even Swift's vice was a sort of virtue in excess. So strong was his hatred of hypocrisy that he carried it to an unfortunate extreme, hiding even the appearance of piety so that he might seem worse than he was: "An abhorrence of hypocrisy was a striking particular in *Swift's* character, but it is difficult to determine whether it was more a virtue than a vice, for it brought upon him the charge of irreligion, and encouraged others to be irreligious" (71). Swift was in fact so secretive about going to church and about conducting prayers at home that "he appeared to neglect both" (72).

In his recasting of Hawkesworth, Johnson totally reverses this emphasis; for Johnson, Swift is first and foremost a writer and only secondarily a clergyman at every stage of his life. While Johnson could pay honest tribute to Swift's conscientious performance of his ecclesiastical duties, perhaps Swift's apparent lack of decorum led Johnson to play down the fact that Swift was a clergyman, thus avoiding the portrayal of a bad example. This speculation is prompted by Johnson's omission of several of Hawkesworth's most effective anecdotes—stories about Swift which at first glance seem irresistible in their potential for being given Johnsonian polish and for revealing character concisely but which involve behavior inappropriate in a clergyman.

Most readers would probably be attracted to Swift's character as it is revealed in Hawkesworth's version of Orrery's anecdote about Swift's first Wednesday service at Laracor. Finding the church empty except for his clerk Roger, "with a composure and gravity that upon this occasion was irresistibly ridiculous, he began, 'Dearly beloved *Roger*, the scripture moveth you and me in sundry places,' and so proceeded to the end of the service" (16). Elsewhere Hawkesworth recounts Orrery's anecdote about Swift's engaging in a footrace to church and running down the aisle to win his wager. But it is all too easy to see why Johnson omitted these anecdotes; in fact, one can hardly imagine Johnson including them. Wagering and waggery in a holy setting were not behaviors he was likely to select for anecdotal display.

An outright revulsion to the subject matter may have governed Johnson's omission of an even more striking anecdote. Those who argue that Johnson's treatment of Swift is unstintingly negative should note that, had Johnson wanted really to pillory

Swift, he could have used the anecdotes just mentioned or the following, still more damaging story about Swift's casual expression of a suicidal wish. At a point late in Swift's life, a large pier glass happened to fall just where Swift and another clergyman had been standing a moment before. The other clergyman remarked that it was fortunate they had moved. "The dean replied, that, as to himself, he was sorry he had changed ground, and wished the glass had fallen upon him" (Hawkesworth 56).

Hawkesworth tells the story as evidence that Swift was a burden to himself and was tired of life. To Johnson, the thought of a suicidal wish expressed by one clergyman to another must have been shocking. This anecdote would have been doubly painful to Johnson, for he had suffered from self-destructive thoughts himself, and might even have been trebly painful because it was rumored that Hawkesworth himself had committed suicide.[7] Thoughts of a departed friend's melancholy end, or, more accurately, the need to avoid such thoughts, might have supplied yet another possible reason for Johnson's omission of this damaging anecdote.

Johnson's relationship with his chief source in Swiftian biography lets us see Johnson the biographical rhetorician at work. His practice is to present as persuasive a view of his subject as he can, and he is encouraged to do so by the presence of an intelligent interlocutor. His treatment of Swift was more than just responsive, however; the example provided by Hawkesworth spurred him on to one of his liveliest biographical efforts, even if it is one of his most unfair. Several of Johnson's strengths are apparent in his reaction to Hawkesworth: his broader, more encompassing sense of irony; his resistance to unqualified praise; his refusal to be impressed by power and celebrity; his skeptical awareness of the mixed nature of human motivation and character. Undeniably, Johnson's weaknesses are also strikingly apparent in the *Life of Swift:* his unfairness, his tendency to distort the truth in the interest of delivering a crushing rejoinder, and his hypersensitivity to unconventional behavior in one whose calling made him an example. But these can be better understood in the context of a dialectical engagement with an illustrious predecessor.

Six

The Probable and the

Marvelous in the

Life of Milton

In both the biographical and the critical portions of Samuel Johnson's *Life of Milton*, critics have often seen signs of ambivalence.[1] Most readers, beginning with Johnson's contemporaries, have found in it plenty of evidence of Johnson's hostility to Milton, which the Hill edition emphasizes by prominently quoting Johnson's remark that there have been "too many honeysuckle lives of Milton" and that his "should be in another strain" (1:84n1). On the other hand, in the *Life* and elsewhere we can also find "sufficient evidence that he admired Milton, while disapproving of Milton idolators" (Brink 495). But the striking contrast between Johnson's apparent bias against Milton and the praise he lavished upon him, I believe, has deflected attention from other more significant ambivalences in his dialectical approach to Milton.

Normally Johnson wields dialectical rhetoric with magisterial skill, so that we come away from the *Lives* feeling that we have actively participated in the pro-and-con movement of his critical

The Probable in the
Life of Milton

and biographical judgments. In the *Life of Milton*, however, he becomes entangled in certain contradictions characteristic of his age, an era which was undergoing a shift in thinking about the concept of probable truth. The older criterion of probable truth, deriving from Aristotelian philosophy, applied the questions "How consistent with well-attested opinion is X?" and "How internally consistent is X?" in order to evaluate the epistemological probability of a statement or a piece of testimony. The newer criterion applied the question "How well supported by evidence is X?" In its uneasy and sometimes contradictory movement between these two concepts, Johnson's *Life of Milton* exemplifies the transition. [2]

There is another type of contradiction in Johnson's manner of drawing probable conclusions in the *Life of Milton:* he applies the truth criterion of consistency itself in contradictory ways, as we all do. On the one hand, we tend to believe a biographical anecdote if it is free from internal contradictions and if it accords with what we already know about the subject; we invoke consistency as a criterion to verify a story's credibility, while inconsistency falsifies it. On the other hand, wherever human testimony is involved, we expect a certain degree of inconsistency. If two witnesses' accounts agree too closely, we become suspicious; similarly, if a supposedly factual narrative is too tidily consistent, we have reason to think that it has been distorted and that some of life's inconsistencies have been suppressed. We extend this principle to our evaluation of fictions, feeling that a too consistent set of behaviors makes a character into a two-dimensional stereotype, while a certain measure of inconsistency or unpredictability gives us a sense of authenticity, a sense of character in the round.

There is finally no way neatly to resolve this contradiction, because the simple truth is that both the existence of consistent

The Philosophical
Biographer

patterns and the existence of divergences from patterns can sometimes reasonably be invoked as criteria of authenticity. In Johnson's day this contradiction seems to have been regarded with
indifference, even though it undermines the validity of such key
literary concepts as the decorum of character, which is essentially
a criterion of consistency.

To some extent, the conflict between opposing truth criteria
was inherent in the seventeenth- and eighteenth-century debate
over the evidences for the Christian faith. When writers invoked
both the argument from design and the argument from miracles,
they were employing these contradictory criteria. As Sir Leslie
Stephen says in his discussion of William Paley's *Evidences of
Christianity* (1794), "From the ingenuity displayed in the watch
we first infer the maker, and then when any unexpected movement takes place, we may assume that the maker is at work"
(1:352). In literary criticism, a parallel contradiction arises: both
design and departure from design are regarded as authenticating
features.

Johnson defines "marvellous" as a term "used, in works of criticism, to express any thing exceeding natural power, opposed to
the *probable*" (*Dictionary*). But in this and in Johnson's other definitions of the term, he dodges a crucial ambiguity: he treats "probable" and "marvelous" as antonyms when the standard usage of
these terms, sanctioned by Addison's example in *Spectator* 315,
makes the marvelous a subcategory of the probable. As Addison
puts it:

> If the Fable be only Probable, it differs nothing from a true His-
> tory; if it is only Marvellous, it is no better than a Romance. The
> great Secret therefore of Heroic Poetry is to relate such Circum-
> stances, as may produce in the Reader at the same time both Be-
> lief and Astonishment. This is brought to pass in a *well chosen*

Fable, by the Account of such Things as have really happen'd, or
at least of such Things as have happened according to the received Opinions of Mankind. [Addison 3:143–44]

The last phrase of Addison's last sentence ("according . . . Mankind") is the traditional definition of "probable," stemming from
Aristotle's *Prior Analytics*.[3]

So although "marvelous" can mean merely "surpassing credit"
(Johnson, *Dictionary*), which makes it synonymous with "incredible" ("surpassing belief"—Johnson, *Dictionary*), usually the term
referred to something credible, not incredible. The term "marvelous" was used to denote precisely such things as are believed
on good authority despite appearances of improbability, just as
the term "miracle" denotes something credited despite its divergence from the normal laws of nature.

Johnson's willingness to overlook the problem of the marvelous in its relationship to probability and consistency leads him
to become entangled in certain contradictions in the critical sections of the *Life of Milton*. Literary conventions are ways of imposing consistency upon experience and shaping it to fit established
patterns of significance, but this sort of consistency can be invoked as a sign of improbability as well as probability. I have
already cited such hypothetical instances as the witnesses whose
stories are too pat or the writer whose characters are so consistent
that we see them as merely two-dimensional stereotypes, but virtually any patterning convention of a literary work can be con-
strued in either way—as authenticating the work or as discredit-
ing it. Fragmentary syntax, for instance, may be taken as an
authenticating sign of emotion in the speaker, but once this feature has been codified by Longinus as a feature of the sublime
style, it becomes potentially artificial, and its conventionality
thereby undermines its credibility.

Just as he does in drawing critical judgments, Johnson uses the criterion of consistency (internal as well as external) in two contradictory ways when he evaluates biographical testimony. Sometimes he takes an account and attacks its probability by showing that it is inconsistent with itself or with external circumstances, but sometimes he attacks an account by arguing that it is too pat and consistent. Parallel to this unresolved contradiction in the biographical technique of the *Life of Milton* runs a similar contradiction in Johnson's constant striving to convert the marvelous into the merely probable. Underlying both forms of contradiction is the incompleteness of the transition already mentioned, between two different views of knowledge and inquiry: the truth is that which is consistent with what we already know about the subject, or the truth is that which is best supported by evidence. In invoking first one and then the other criterion without being conscious of, or at any rate distressed by, the contradiction, Johnson typifies the transitional character of the age in which he lived, caught between two paradigms of knowledge.[4] However, at several points Johnson sees Milton as managing to fuse these qualities, thereby rising above the Augustan polarities. In describing Milton in this way, Johnson anticipated the Romantics, who formulated a more inclusive concept of probability.[5]

As the frequency of words like "wonder" and "marvel" indicates, the opposition of the probable and the marvelous is in fact a controlling theme of the biography as a whole and is one of the ways in which its author "actively sought to connect Milton's life and art" (Fix, "Distant Genius" 245). Just as Johnson directed much of his literary criticism not so much against Milton as against "critics . . . [he] probably considered adversaries," so in the biographical portions of the *Life*, Johnson worked against the Milton idolatry of the biographers and against the consequent mythologizing of Milton's life.[6]

The Probable in the
Life of Milton

Much of what has been seen as hostility to Milton is really hostility to the notion of biographical marvels. Johnson clearly felt that Milton's readers, with the help of the biographers, were unjustifiably turning their hero into a prodigy and a wonder, so he set about converting the marvelous into the merely probable. Many aspects of Milton's life that might contribute to our seeing him as an embodiment of marvelous or heroic virtue are subjected to withering scrutiny by means of a sarcastic Johnsonian rhetoric that enforces acts of judgment and comparison. One result is that, when Johnson does finally pay tribute to Milton's genuine hero- ism, the praise is entirely credible; another result is that the reader is engaged in processes of judgment that work against his uncritical willingness to marvel.

In eighteenth-century terms, one of the potential responses to a wonder was called "admiration" (from MF *admirer*, Latin *ad-* + *mirari*, to wonder), a term which then possessed negative as well as positive connotations. At the positive end of the scale, admira- tion could be (but, as Paul Alkon has reminded us, need not be) associated with an aesthetic but rational sensitivity to sublimity: "Johnson's predecessors often associated admiration with wonder and astonishment as responses evoked by those qualities in an epic, whatever they might be, which were identified as sublime." But at the other end of the range of meanings (and Johnson was sensitive to the word's negative connotations), admiration could be an irrational response, an astonished suspension of judgment caused by something "beyond the boundaries of the naturally es- tablished order" (Alkon, "Admiration" 62, 73).

Johnson also attacks admiration because it is not only poten- tially irrational but affected and insincere as well. Johnson's fa- mous statement that *"Paradise Lost* is one of the books which the reader admires and lays down, and forgets to take up again" (1:183) is less an ambivalent comment on the poem than a satiric comment on its readers: much of the admiration directed at the poem, Johnson implies, is felt because that is the fashionable response. If the reader's admiration were both more rational and more genuine, one supposes, the book would not so soon be laid down and forgotten.

In checking our tendencies toward admiration and uncritical wonder, Johnson usually proceeds by indirection, so that tone and attitude often suggest the movement from marvels to mere probabilities. Since tone is by its very nature ambiguous and unprovable, ambiguities arise from the subtlety of Johnson's technique. For example, according to biographical tradition, Milton was supposed to have read "all the Greek and Latin writers" (1:91) during his five years of residence at his father's estate, which leads Johnson to ask: "With what limitations this universality is to be understood who shall inform us?" The implication is of course that there must have been limitations, but they can never be known. Johnson exploits the momentary suspension and sense of doubt created by this question to strike a note of mild sarcasm as he begins the next paragraph: "It might be supposed that he who read so much should have done nothing else; but Milton found time to write the masque of *Comus*" (1:92). Whatever its tone, this statement entails a comparative weighing of probabilities to show that Milton's accomplishment, however great, was not superhuman. The indirection of Johnson's technique leaves room for ambiguity, but only within the limits of a general movement away from wonder and toward calm understanding.

Less ambiguous examples of Johnson's use of sarcasm to enforce our concern with probability may be found in his frequent use of reductive analogies. He feels that Milton's earlier biographers were absurd in their wish to find extraordinary virtue even in Milton's becoming a schoolteacher; Phillips, for instance, extenuated Milton's humble vocation by claiming that Milton taught only the children of relatives and friends, clearly aiming to suggest that he was remarkably free from greedy or self-serving motives. Johnson uses a sarcastically reductive analogy to show that the "extenuation" is more degrading than what it aims to excuse: "He did not sell literature to all comers at an open shop [in Phillips's account]; he was a chamber-milliner, and measured his commodities only to his friends" (1:109).

Johnson's mockery of Phillips does not end there; in making fun of Phillips's intention to puff Milton by "invest[ing] him with military splendour," Johnson mimics Phillips's language: "An event cannot be set at a much greater distance than by having been only *designed, about some time,* if a man *be not much mistaken.* Milton shall be a pedagogue no longer; for, if Philips [*sic*] be not much mistaken, somebody at some time designed him for a soldier" (1:109–10). In such passages, one feels that Johnson's sarcasm is belabored and overdone; his debunking attacks on the biographers go too far afield. However, it is easy to cite cases in which Johnson directs his sarcasm against Milton—more specifically, against Milton's own sense that he was a prodigy and a marvel.

Milton published his own juvenilia, for instance, presuming that his early work showed extraordinary promise. But Johnson says sarcastically at one point that Milton published a juvenile poem in an unfinished state "because he was 'nothing satisfied with what he had done,' supposing his readers less nice than himself" (1:161). One is reminded that the tradition of biographical Milton-idolatry began with Milton himself.

Throughout the early pages of the *Life of Milton*, Johnson continues this attack on the poet's belief in his own youthful precociousness. He carries this off by implicitly comparing a set of parallel examples—an essentially inductive and probabilistic mode of argument. Noting that Milton recorded the dates of composition of his early writings, Johnson immediately invokes comparative criteria by remarking that the recording of dates is itself

"a boast of which the learned Politian had given him an example,"
adding that Cowley is one of "many" who outdid Milton in "vernal fertility (1:87)."

While the form of the argument is encouraging us to draw
probable judgments based on comparison, the language is indirectly prejudging the case for us. In the phrase "vernal fertility,"
Johnson mocks Milton's pretension by letting his own diction tip
delicately toward the ponderous and by letting its metaphoric implications work against any sense of the marvelous: we expect
springtime to be fertile. In the next breath, Johnson again con-
verts a marvel into an ordinary probability by sweeping us along
to a more humble standard of comparison, the school: Milton's
early versifications of two Psalms "would in any numerous school
have obtained praise, but not excited wonder" (1:87).

Similarly, Milton's university exercises are mentioned because
he later published some of them, but within the same paragraph
in which Johnson cites these, he tells us that Milton was not liked
by his college fellows and seems to take "a certain demure pleasure" (Fogle 26) in recounting the story that Milton was "one of
the last students in either university that suffered the publick in-
dignity of corporal correction" (1:88). Johnson's intentions cannot
be demonstrated, but one of the advantages of his sometimes casual handling of narrative transitions is that it allows the seemingly chance juxtaposition of elements that are perhaps placed
together on purpose: the ambitious young man, proud of his own
poetry, gets his comeuppance in the form of a public whipping.
Whether intentional or not, this reduction of the marvelous by
means of a commonplace and undignified context is a return to
the probable—with a vengeance.

Equally reductive is Johnson's treatment of Milton's belief in
the marvel of inspiration: according to Richardson, Milton would
be seized occasionally by a poetical "oestrum" (1:138) during
which he would compose rapidly and with little effort, calling his

daughter to write down what he recited. To treat such a phenomenon as a marvel is to hint that it is divinely inspired and
hence to overestimate its importance; certainly belief in divine
inspiration, like belief in "enthusiasm," can take the form of the
sin of pride. Johnson takes care, therefore, to work in precisely
the opposite direction, reducing this "marvel" by placing it in the
context of ordinary manual crafts, letting his diction descend
from the dignified to the colloquial:

> These bursts of lights and involutions of darkness, these transient
> and involuntary excursions and retrocessions of invention, having
> some appearance of deviation from the common train of Nature,
> are eagerly caught by the lovers of a wonder. Yet something of
> this inequality happens to every man in every mode of exertion,
> manual or mental. The mechanick cannot handle his hammer and
> his file at all times with equal dexterity; there are hours, he knows
> not why, when "his hand is out." [1:139]

Johnson goes on to challenge the authenticity of this "marvel" by
pointing out an inconsistent circumstance in Richardson's account: how could Milton's daughter have been "called to secure
what came" (1:138), when it is said elsewhere that she was never
taught to write, and that for this reason Milton used to ask visitors
to transcribe for him? In any case, Milton's bursts of creativity,
Johnson suggests, resulted from Milton's long practice in blank
verse, making composition "prompt and habitual" when the
mood was right (1:139).

A similar and related marvel that Johnson attacks is the idea
that Milton's creativity increased and diminished seasonally; this
notion, Johnson says, "may . . . justly be derided as the fumes of
vain imagination" (1:137). It is the deterministic quality of the
idea that bothers him; human endeavor depends upon hope, and
the idea of seasonal influence surrenders hope to "a cross wind or
a cloudy sky" or to the power of suggestion: "while this notion has

possession of the head, it produces the inability which it supposes" (1:137). A similar delusion, in Johnson's view, is the notion that earlier historical periods or other geographical regions might have been more favorable to creativity than England in the seventeenth century. Johnson conflates all these notions in his sarcastic phraseology: "Among this lagging race of frosty grovellers he might still have risen into eminence by producing something which 'they should not willingly let die.' However inferior to the heroes who were born in better ages, he might still be great among his contemporaries, with the hope of growing every day greater in the dwindle of posterity: he might still be the giant of the pygmies, the one-eyed monarch of the blind" (1:138). Again, the sarcasm is perhaps somewhat disproportionate to the idea that gave rise to it, but it is entertaining and amusing.

While Johnson does finally express admiration for Milton's strength of character, he nevertheless deemphasizes the notion that Milton was a political hero. For example, he denies that Milton was ever in danger at the time of the Restoration. At one point he tells an anecdote in which Milton supposedly saved Davenant's life during the Puritan rebellion, and Davenant later saved Milton's in return; Johnson undercuts its credibility, first by calling attention to its third- or fourth-hand provenance and second by calling it "a reciprocation of generosity and gratitude so pleasing that the tale makes its own way to credit" (1:129). Johnson's rather dubious implication is that a story with such extraordinary moral symmetry is inherently implausible because its pleasing quality makes it likely to be passed on even if it is false. In this instance the story is too "pat" to be likely.

Elsewhere Johnson recounts what he calls "an obscure story" (1:131) to the effect that Milton received an offer of court employment under Charles II but turned it down because he wanted "to live and die an honest man" (1:131). Johnson includes the anecdote, perhaps because it shows Milton as self-righteously anti-Royalist, but he regards the story as improbable, first because of lack of supporting evidence, and second because "large offers and sturdy rejections are among the most common topicks of falsehood" (1:132). This second basis for rejecting the story is similar to the criterion used in undercutting the Davenant anecdote. Superficially, Johnson seems to be saying simply that this is the kind of story that is frequently fabricated. But a closer look shows that such a story, in Milton's case, has been credited because of its consistency with the previous biographers' portrait of Milton as the embodiment of personal integrity. This is the sort of flattering anecdote upon which they fastened; anyone eager to establish Milton's integrity would be sure to quote it. In this instance too Johnson rejected an anecdote on the implicit grounds that it had the consistency and appropriateness of a good fiction.

Of course, Johnson had good cause to be suspicious of the mythologizing tendencies of the earlier biographers, who looked for marvelous and heroic virtue even in the humblest circumstances of Milton's life. Jonathan Richardson, for instance, not only compares Milton to Hercules but places him in an even more heroic context drawn from Scripture:

> He Forsook all These Endearments to come Hither, where War was Kindling apace, to Assist with the Utmost of his Abilities on the Side where He judg'd Truth was. if any had said to him as the Elder Brother of *David* said to that *Stripling*. 1 Sam. xvii. 28, 29. *Why camest thou down Hither? and with Whom hast thou left those few Sheep in the Wilderness? I know thy Pride, and the Naughtiness of thine Heart, for thou art come down that thou mightst see the Battle.* he would have Answer'd as *David; What have I now done? is there not a Cause?* [Darbishire, *Early Lives* 216–17]

Contrast Johnson's treatment of Milton's return to England:

The Philosophical
Biographer

Let not our veneration for Milton forbid us to look with some
degree of merriment on great promises and small performance, on
the man who hastens home because his countrymen are contend-
ing for their liberty, and, when he reaches the scene of action,
vapours away his patriotism in a private boarding-school. This is
the period of his life from which all his biographers seem inclined
to shrink. [1:99]

(Oddly, Johnson fails to notice the incongruity between his own
statement that Milton decided to "hasten home" and, in the same
paragraph, that Milton "staid two months more at Rome" [1:96,
97].)

Johnson notes that, when faced with Milton's less than heroic
employment as a schoolmaster, the biographers responded by
fabricating marvels: that Milton taught for free, that he taught
merely for the love of learning, and "that in the art of education
he performed wonders" (1:99). Johnson's rejoinder is a probable
argument based on comparison and personal experience: any
teacher knows "how much patience it requires to recall vagrant
inattention, to stimulate sluggish indifference, and to rectify absurd misapprehension" (1:99). Johnson blames the biographers'
exaggerations upon their desire "to excuse an act which no wise
man will consider as in itself disgraceful" (1:98). But another way
of stating the case is to say that the biographers were betrayed
into this sort of falsehood because they were aiming at a truth
based on consistency: how could our hero do something so unheroic? A decorum of character lies behind their supposed falsehoods: Milton must be extraordinary in everything he does.

Johnson is attacking their falsely negative view of the calling of
schoolmaster, but in doing so, he has it both ways: he denies that
Milton needs to be excused for teaching, but he also sees teaching
as pretty trivial when weighed against the civil strife that supposedly brought Milton back to England. Johnson's sarcasm is

two-edged in another sense: his phrase "this wonder-working academy" strikes first at the biographers' overestimation of Milton but then turns against Milton's supposed concept of an academy that accelerated the study of the classics and embodied educational reform by focusing more closely on natural philosophy. This attack on "wonder-working" reforms, which incidentally distorts Milton's real concept of education (Fix, "Distant Genius" 246), gives rise to a discussion of the impracticability of such schemes, culminating in the aphorism "we are perpetually moralists, but we are geometricians only by chance" (1:100). The overall effect is subtly contradictory: Johnson associates Milton with a false individualism that flies in the face of the wisdom of consensus even while Johnson's own probabilistic mode of argument entails a constant, individualistic resistance to consensus.

Johnson's treatment of Milton's dispute with Salmasius pursues a similar antithetical course. Sentence by sentence, Johnson first arouses our expectation that we will hear marvels and then systematically deflates these expectations by calling attention to the prosaic and ordinary grounds for his own probable conclusions, which run counter to the consensus established by biographical tradition. Enlisted in a controversy over one of the great questions of the day, Salmasius brought to the defense of monarchy a degree of wisdom, learning, and skill "almost exceeding all hope of human attainment," coupled with "expedition in writing" that was "wonderful," as Johnson phrases it, using unironic and unqualified hyperbole (1:111–12). But Milton's tract, Johnson says, attacked Salmasius on trivial grounds: as Johnson puts it reductively, "the rights of nations and of kings sink into questions of grammar, if grammarians discuss them" (1:113). Nevertheless, Milton's tract was better received than Salmasius's, probably, Johnson argues, because Salmasius argued for a "stale doctrine of authority" and was himself so much an established authority that everyone was happy to see him "defied and insulted by a new name" (1:114); the inductive basis for this argument is our general experience of the human hunger for innovation. Johnson's persuasive strategy is to associate Milton with a perverse human tendency to rebel against the wisdom of consensus.

Throughout this narrative episode, the language of probable argument ("as was reported," "probably," "unable to decide," "in my opinion," "is very credible," "there is not much proof," "might incline," "if I remember right," "perhaps," "commonly said"—all drawn from a seven-paragraph section, 1:111–15) runs parallel to the language of sarcastic deflation, so that a movement from the marvelous to the probable is expressed by a movement from the dignified to the undignified.

Johnson engages in a rather extended argument to undercut another marvel: the "slow sale and tardy reputation" of *Paradise Lost* (1:142). "Have not lamentation and wonder been lavished on an evil that was never felt?" Johnson asks. Then he probabilistically measures the apparently slow progress of the book against the circumstances that made such a slow pace likely: public praise for a "defender of regicides" was unlikely in Charles's reign, for one thing, and for another, literacy was less widespread, so that editions were generally smaller than in the eighteenth century. (Here, in his best probabilistic manner, Johnson does a bit of computation, comparing the slow sale of *Paradise Lost* to the slow sale of Shakespeare's works.) Having weighed and compared, Johnson concludes that the book's reception was not a marvel by virtue of its slowness; in fact, its sale was actually unusually quick: "The sale of thirteen hundred copies in two years, in opposition to so much recent enmity and to a style of versification new to all and disgusting to many, was an uncommon example of the prevalence of genius" (1:144). The poem that seemed a marvelous example of fame's tardiness proves to be an "uncommon" but not improbable instance of fame's promptness instead.

The Probable in the
Life of Milton

In all of these instances of his undercutting of the marvels perpetuated by Milton's biographers, we feel the pressure of Johnson's skepticism and resistance to spurious authority. He engages us in the process of judgment by constantly invoking comparisons and by calling attention to the concept of degrees of probability, so that we participate in a critical revision of the biographical tradition. As I have suggested, implicit in this revision is a shift in the notion of probable truth itself, away from the idea that probability inheres in a consensus of authorities and toward the idea that probability inheres in an act of individual judgment that evaluates evidence by juxtaposing and weighing degrees of likelihood.

Paradoxically, though, while engaging us in the process of asserting individual judgment against consensus views, Johnson shows us that Milton himself represents the dangers of such self-assertion. Johnson pays tribute to Milton's resolute individualism, but he is also acutely aware of its hazards—chief among them being the risk that, without consensus as a corrective, imagination can too easily distort individual judgment. One form this distortion can take is an overestimation of oneself and a corresponding underestimation of others. Another form it can take is mere unconventionality for its own sake.

In portraying Milton as excessively reliant upon his own judgment, Johnson's literary and political outlooks intersect, for the role of individual judgment in relation to authority and consensus is a problem common to both. "Milton's republicanism seems to Johnson clearly linked with the other antisocial attitudes he discerns in Milton's life and tends to confirm his observations on Milton's character" (Fix, "Distant Genius" 250).

On the other hand, anyone who would work marvels must be independent, and Johnson persuasively portrays Milton as admirably secure in his sense of self-esteem. Early applause "exalted him in his own opinion" (1:94), but his sense of independence and supe-riority was justified; he showed "not with ostentatious exultation, but with calm confidence, his high opinion of his own powers" (1:102), framing a promise to achieve something great, a promise Johnson finds "at once fervid, pious, and rational" (1:203).

Johnson moves in both directions in treating Milton's self-re-liance, as though trying to exemplify the striking of a balanced judgment. A sense of one's worth and potential is valuable as long as it takes into account the need to be subservient to God's will and to study and prepare oneself—key qualities of the promise Johnson endorses. Furthermore, Milton's sense of worth was jus-tified by his accurate judgment of his own abilities. He was spurred on by "such expectations as naturally arose from the sur-vey of his attainments and the consciousness of his powers" (1:134). This gave Milton a quality of imperturbability that John-son admires. He imagines the author of *Paradise Lost* as "calm and confident, little disappointed, not at all dejected, relying on his own merit with steady consciousness, and waiting without impa-tience the vicissitudes of opinion and the impartiality of a future generation" (1:144).

On the other hand, in several places in the narrative, Milton's self-esteem is linked with foolish disregard for rightful authority and with deceptive fantasies or imaginings. Johnson sees Milton's republicanism merely as an egotistical hatred of authority and his political career as an exercise in self-importance: at one point, Johnson writes, Milton's imagination misled him into the "fan-tastical" thought "that the nation, agitated as it was [just prior to the Restoration], might be settled by a pamphlet" from his hand (1:125). Similarly, just as Charles was about to be restored, Milton feared for his own safety "and, proportioning his sense of danger to his opinion of the importance of his writings, thought it convenient to seek some shelter" (1:126–27). Worse still, Johnson

says, the fantastic element in Milton's sense of self-worth led to contempt for others: "It appears in all his writings that he had the usual concomitant of great abilities, a lofty and steady confidence in himself, perhaps not without some contempt of others; for scarcely any man ever wrote so much and praised so few. Of his praise he was very frugal, as he set its value high; and considered his mention of a name as a security against the waste of time and a certain preservative against oblivion" (1:94). This aims to be a carefully balanced treatment or at least one in which unbalance is effectively concealed. Milton's sense of self-worth seems praise-worthy in the connotations of "lofty and steady," but "contempt" carries us in the other direction. "Frugal," "value," and "security" impart negative mercantile connotations, suggesting that Milton was engaged in a sort of commerce, unable to distribute praise without exhausting his main stock of self-esteem. At odds with these connotations of penny-pinching are the religious connotations of the final phrases; as Johnson never forgets, there is no "certain preservative against oblivion," no real "security against the waste of time" except eternal salvation. Thus our evaluation of Milton is complicated by the way Johnson injects moral considerations into what is finally a question of literary judgment.[7] The disproportion of Milton's judgments, his lack of a sense of what is fitting in praise and dispraise, is suggested by the collision of monetary and religious frames of reference in the connotations of Johnson's figurative language. Johnson's language works to involve us in Milton's judgments, showing that they are distorted and compromised.

Johnson's critical judgments in the *Life of Milton* are also complicated by his ambivalent treatment of the function of generic conventions. On the one hand, he is capable of evaluating *Paradise Lost* in part by measuring its conformity to the conventions of epic poetry; on the other hand, he condemns *Lycidas* for the im-

The Philosophical
Biographer

probability which results precisely from its conformity with the conventions of pastoral poetry, a genre whose "inherent improbability always forces dissatisfaction on the mind" (1:163). Johnson's implicit standard of judgment is the degree of correspondence between the feeling and the utterance, a direct sign-state relationship that does not allow for the intermediate role of convention. Here then is another manifestation of the dilemma of applying consistency as a test of truth: formal, artificial, highly patterned discourse calls itself into doubt. If an expression of grief is too careful an embodiment of conventions, then it is disqualified through lack of sincerity. Just as the probability of an anecdote can be undermined by its artfulness, a poem too finely wrought and too carefully placed in its generic conventions is no marvel; it is merely unbelievable. Johnson has not forgotten or "neglected to remember" the artifice and convention involved in the pastoral; he has written "sound criticism that went to the heart of the matter" in his critique of *Lycidas*.[8] Unfortunately, the heart of the matter is an ambiguity inherent in the problematic relationship between an utterance and the conventions that give it shape.

Another reason for Johnson's distrust of generic convention, Leopold Damrosch suggests, "is that he sees it as an excuse not to know what one means. Whereas modern theorists tend to see genre as a type of the communal code that makes understanding possible, Johnson sees it as a conventional pattern that enables writers to imitate other writers instead of confronting life directly."[9]

Johnson's failure to allow for the role of convention in mediating between feeling and utterance is evident in his criticism of *Comus*, which is unanswerable and amusing but ultimately unfair. He treats this highly artificial masque as though it should live up to the criteria of probability we would invoke in judging a realistic drama:

The Probable in the
Life of Milton

As a drama it is deficient. The action is not probable. A Masque, in those parts where supernatural intervention is admitted, must indeed be given up to all the freaks of imagination; but so far as the action is merely human it ought to be reasonable, which can hardly be said of the conduct of the two brothers, who, when their sister sinks with fatigue in a pathless wilderness, wander both away in search of berries too far to find their way back, and leave a helpless Lady to all the sadness and danger of solitude. This however is a defect overbalanced by its convenience. [1:168]

Johnson is on more solid ground in his magisterial treatment of *Paradise Lost*. Here he manages to arrive at a synthesis of several criteria of probability which are elsewhere held in awkward and contradictory antithesis: "Of the *probable* and the *marvellous*, two parts of a vulgar epick poem which immerge the critick in deep consideration, the *Paradise Lost* requires little to be said. It contains the history of a miracle, of Creation and Redemption; it displays the power and the mercy of the Supreme Being: the probable therefore is marvellous, and the marvellous is probable" (1:174). The "inconvenience" of the subject matter is that it evades our attempts to test its truth against our experience; since Adam and Eve "are in a state which no other man or woman can ever know," this places a limit upon our "curiosity or sympathy" (1:181). True, we are involved by our interest in our own salvation or damnation, but we have already thought about these ultimate concerns, and we gain no really new imaginative experience from Milton's images of heaven and hell. In fact, Johnson argues, we are overwhelmed by the greatness of the cosmic forces of good and evil, so that "the mind sinks under them in passive helplessness, content with calm belief and humble adoration" (1:182) rather than participating actively. However, the realm of "known truths" can arouse our deepest interest, and Milton moves confidently in this realm, assimilating a vast range of materials drawn

The Philosophical
Biographer

from the whole range of human knowledge, "with judgement to digest and fancy to combine them" (1:183).

The movement of this argument is pro and con, for and against a favorable evaluation based on degrees of imaginative participation in the poem, but the pro-and-con subarguments are related to the opposition of the unknown to the known and the marvelous to the probable. The realm of the unknown, the fanciful, is sublime, great, expansive, and powerful—but not directly related to our everyday experience. The realm of the known—"the few radical positions which the Scriptures afforded him"—is more directly relevant but must "be conveyed to the mind by a new train of intermediate images" in order to strike the mind vividly (1:183, 182). Milton managed to convey it through his assimilation of the entire range of human knowledge, which furnished him with an almost limitless supply of materials with which to diversify and amplify his work. The result is a poem in which the marvelous and the probable are united: our imagination is stirred by marvels, but our judgment is exercised by the deployment of a "train of intermediate images" embodying probability.

When Milton fails, Johnson implies, it is a failure to live up to either criterion of truth. On the one hand, there is too little for us to test against our own experience: "The want of human interest is always felt" (1:183). On the other hand, there are failures of internal consistency. Johnson follows John Clarke and John Dennis in objecting to the "inconsistent materiality of angels."[10] Having been forced to endow spiritual beings with bodily form, Milton "should have secured the consistency of his system by keeping immateriality out of sight." But instead Milton's demons and angels "are sometimes pure spirit and sometimes animated body" (1:184). Similarly, Milton had difficulty excluding from the thoughts of the newly created Adam such ideas as only a man in society, and in a fallen state, could conceive (1:186–87).

The Probable in the
Life of Milton

Finally, in his treatment of "L'Allegro" and "Il Penseroso" Johnson touches upon another way of synthesizing the old and the new truth criteria, the truth of consistency and the truth of experience: "The author's design is not, what Theobald has remarked, merely to shew how objects derived their colours from the mind, by representing the operation of the same things upon the gay and the melancholy temper, or upon the same man as he is differently disposed; but rather how, among the successive variety of appearances, every disposition of mind takes hold on those by which it may be gratified" (1:165–66). In speaking of a "train of intermediate images" that conveys truth to the mind, and in referring to "the operation of the same things upon the gay and the melancholy temper," Johnson is operating within a Lockean set of assumptions; he is thinking of the impingement of sensory data upon the mind by means of intermediate ideas. But Johnson briefly goes beyond the solipsistic notion of the mind as passive recipient. In his analysis of "L'Allegro" and "Il Penseroso," he emphasizes that the point is not merely the coloring of experiences by moods; rather, each state of mind searches for objects that gratify it. The mind is not merely the passive recipient of experience; the imagination hungrily seeks out truths appropriate to its emotional and cognitive state. Here, however glancingly, Johnson anticipates the Romantics' emphasis upon the imagination's active and selective power, so that criteria of consistency and experience become complementary aspects of a single thing.

Throughout the *Life of Milton*, Johnson makes various and sometimes contradictory use of the association of the marvelous with the rare, the remote, and the unusual, in contrast to the association of the probable with consensus, the near at hand, and the everyday. Milton's confident individualism is thus ambivalently linked with his capacity for the marvelous and the sublime. Johnson strives for balanced judgment by conveying admiration of Milton's independence while simultaneously noting its dan-

The Philosophical
Biographer

gers. Through his irony and skepticism, Johnson subtly associates himself and his judgments both with the notion of consensus and with the notion of judging by evidence and experience; in this ambivalence he typifies the Augustan age. Yet in trying to do justice to the independent, solitary, creative genius who created his own world and refused to be overly influenced by consensus views, Johnson sounds pre-Romantic, anticipating the doctrines of sincerity and the imagination's active and selective power.

Seven

Judgment and the

Art of Contrast

in the

Life of Pope

Johnson's masterpiece of dialectical rhetoric is his *Life of Pope*, in which he uses contrastive patterns of thought to enforce carefully qualified biographical judgments and to involve the reader in actively preferring one interpretation to another. The *Life of Pope* shows that, far from being mechanical and inflexible, dialectic is an instrument that Johnson creatively adapts to his improvisational twists and turns of thought.

The adaptability of Johnson's contrastive rhetoric can be seen better in the *Life of Pope* than in any of his other biographies. All of the dialectical techniques that Johnson first used in his *Life of Savage* and later perfected in the *Lives of the Poets*—the reversals, the skepticism, the pressure to argue and resist—all these features of his biographical method reach full development in the *Life of Pope*. In fact, exactly this triumph of dialectic gives the *Life* its remark-

The Philosophical
Biographer

able consistency and its structural integrity. In his dialectical mode of inquiry and judgment in the *Life of Pope*, Johnson achieved one of the best and fullest applications of probabilistic rhetoric in a historical period characterized by that rhetoric's flourishing development.

As Johnson conceives of it, judgment is the key faculty for a biographer or historian, since it enables him to reach the truth by weighing juxtaposed probabilities in the absence of intuitive or demonstrative proof. Johnson's several definitions of "judgment" comprise moral, religious, judicial, literary, and epistemological meanings, but the key terms used in his definitions in his *Dictionary* can be conflated to suggest Johnson's Lockean sense of the word's scope: he sees "judgment" as denoting a faculty that *decides* questions of *opinion* by means of *discerning* or *distinguishing* relationships between ideas; it includes the *critical faculty* which evaluates *propriety* or *impropriety* in literature.[1] I am suggesting that biography may have appealed to Johnson partly because it posed an epistemological and rhetorical challenge in the exercise of judgment: it was a new genre, inherently probabilistic and inductive, addressed to a popular audience as well as to a learned one and lacking any clearly defined rhetorical conventions. It invited exploration; it needed a rhetoric of its own. Johnson virtually invented a rhetoric of biography, and one of its distinctive features was an art of contrast deriving from a specific way of encouraging the reader to think about judgment. Since biographical judgment employs a weighing of opposed probabilities, Johnson tends to work dialectically in constructing probable arguments.

The idea of judgment not only influenced Johnson's rhetorical techniques but also guided his biographical inquiries. Questions involving the judgment of opposed probabilities tended to activate a set of powerful, well-integrated, habitual responses in Johnson's writing, and these were more than just mannerisms;

they were the logical, rhetorical, stylistic, and characterological embodiments of a dialectical mode of thought. In Johnson's hands, dialectical opposition became a master principle, governing both the invention of probable arguments and the deployment of expressive devices. Diction, syntax, paragraph structure, narrative shifts, shifts between modes of discourse, shifts from one level of generality to another or from one tone to another, and even the introduction of literary allusions—all tend to cohere by means of patterns of dialectical opposition, as I shall attempt to show.

Despite the seeming finality of many of his statements, Johnson's skeptical, argumentative ethos entails a willingness to suspend judgment and to weigh dialectical opposites before reaching conclusions about human performances. "Johnson's *Lives* are notably reserved about drawing conclusions," Lawrence Lipking observes. "They tend not to speculate about the 'meaning' or ultimate happiness of the lives they survey" ("Johnson and the Meaning of Life" 15). Another recent study suggests that even Johnson's treatment of death is marked by a sort of suspension of judgment, as though Johnson had "refused to employ death as an instrument for delivering either a theological or even a moral verdict on his subjects" (Grundy, "Johnson Looks at Death" 264–65).

This ethos of shying from a verdict, this willingness to argue a case on two sides, calls attention to itself through words that signal probable, rather than demonstrative, argument: "probably," "likely," "perhaps," "seems," etc. Whenever Johnson approaches a delicate, ambiguous topic requiring tact, one notices that he projects a credible ethos by using frequent qualifiers calling attention to judgments: "they may be supposed," "nor do I remember," "in some degree," "seem," "it must be remembered," "he might have," "I know not," "It is indeed not easy to distinguish," "may be said" (3:158–60).

The Philosophical
Biographer

When Johnson does render a verdict, he achieves fairness and credibility by using strategies of restraint like those seen in the *Life of Savage*, seeming to hold back potentially harsh attacks and ending instead with praise: "Pope in his edition [of Shakespeare] undoubtedly did many things wrong, and left many things undone; but let him not be defrauded of his due praise: he was the first that knew, at least the first that told, by what helps the text might be improved" (3:139). Here Johnson establishes his reliability by making a concession dialectically opposed to his main point; he even gives the balance beam a final, judicious tap by means of an inserted self-correction: "at least the first that told." In a number of places in the *Life of Pope*, Johnson further creates an impression that his judgments are reliable by setting them alongside the intemperate judgments of other critics. Through such contrasts and tensions, Johnson creates an ethos of self-restraint.

Throughout the *Life of Pope* this ethos of magisterial fair-mindedness is conveyed by Johnson's familiar alternations of praise and blame. But while the dialectical movements are often simple and obvious enough, the overall effect of such alternations can be quite complex and subtle, as close analysis will show.

Johnson consistently contrasts the personal side of Pope's life, where his weaknesses show clearly, with the public side, where his strengths appear. At one point this practice enables Johnson to resolve an essentially personal question, Pope's degree of education, by shifting to a public perspective. Johnson answers the question of Pope's education by attacking the attackers. Pope's denigrators, he implies, were jealous public onlookers eager "to find that he was not perfect." On the contrary, Johnson argues, Pope's works show him "excursive, vigorous, and diligent, eager to pursue knowledge, and attentive to retain it" (3:216). As Johnson goes on in this celebrated passage to use a metaphor of flight

Judgment in the
Life of Pope

to suggest the quality of Pope's mind, the metaphor also initiates a
contrastive shift in Johnson's perspective, moving from the anecdotal level, with its potentially trivializing attention to the details
of Pope's personal life, and rising to the critical level—a lofty
perspective from which we can see Pope's soaring preeminence as
a poet whose mind was "perpetually on the wing" (3:216), "in its
highest flights still wishing to be higher" (3:217), continuing
"longer on the wing" than Dryden's, "never fall[ing] below" his
admiring readers' expectations (3:223), yet "never elevated to neg-
ligence" (3:218). Johnson carries us, figuratively speaking, from
grotto to open sky.

Furthermore, as Johnson discusses Pope's genius, he establishes another contrast, between opposite virtues: on the one hand
we have poetic "good sense," which is "a sedate and quiescent
quality" (3:217), and on the other we have genius, an active and
aspiring hunger for knowledge and accomplishment. Johnson
shows us how Pope fuses these qualities, joining "poetical prudence" and imaginative freedom. Pope's creativity becomes a perfect instance of dynamic equilibrium.

This dialectical evaluation in turn gives rise to a comparison of
Pope and Dryden, which Johnson sets up in the traditional contrastive pattern supplied by a long line of precedents, ranging from
Longinus's comparison of Demosthenes and Cicero, through Dryden's comparison of Shakespeare and Jonson, to Pope's comparison
of Homer and Virgil in his preface to the *Iliad*. Thus Johnson manages an elegantly complimentary turn in the delicate adjudication
of praise and blame, characterizing Pope and Dryden by using the
dialectical format sanctioned by their own prior usage. He even
uses phraseology that specifically echoes Pope's preface to the *Iliad*
(Smallwood, "Johnson's *Life of Pope*" 50).

As it proceeds, Johnson's comparison of Pope and Dryden becomes still more complex, because the bases for praise and blame

undergo a series of subtle dialectical shifts of their own. In comparatively weighing Pope's "understanding and . . . discernment" against Dryden's, Johnson first opposes judgment and the application of judgment: "Pope had perhaps the judgment of Dryden; but Dryden certainly wanted the diligence of Pope" (3:220, 222). Johnson contrasts innate abilities with "acquired knowledge"; next he contrasts Dryden's general knowledge with Pope's sense of detail; then he contrasts Dryden's and Pope's prose and poetry, weighing Dryden's prose against Pope's by means of an accelerating series of figurative comparisons; and finally he contrasts their degrees of poetic genius, terminating the deliberative pattern with a slight tipping of the scales: "the superiority must, with some hesitation, be allowed to Dryden" (3:222). But the scales shift and seem in the end to balance as Johnson considers the differences of occasion and temperament in the two poets' cases, and he concludes with a comparison that modifies the entire process of judgment: "Dryden is read with frequent astonishment, and Pope with perpetual delight" (3:223). The effect is to remind us that pleasure is a fundamental criterion of judgment, as though Johnson is disentangling us from the complexities of his evaluation and encouraging a return to responses.

Throughout this beautifully constructed evaluation, we may disagree with Johnson's critical judgments, but we endorse his manner of proceeding by means of evaluative contrasts; the ethos is entirely credible and persuasive. The alternation of praise and blame is no merely mechanical device in this passage. In fact, it tends creatively to fuse the complex polarities upon which it plays: we feel that, as the biographer tries to draw judgments worthy of his subject, judgment is constantly returning to that delight for which criticism tries to account. Pope, the soul of decorum and correctness, becomes also an embodiment of the sublime and the imaginative; he achieves a fusion of judgment and imagination which Johnson attributes to *genius* or *wit*.[2] If the Johnsonian ethos strikes the reader as vigorous but thoughtful, argumentative but balanced, lively but deliberate, one crucial reason is the presence of Johnson's dialectical and antithetical mode of judgment, a critical tool which he adapts to many uses.

Aside from providing a consistent yet flexible pattern for the generation of arguments, dialectic has several other logical functions for Johnson. As the Pope-Dryden comparison shows, it serves as a guide to literary evaluation.[3] It also serves as a guide to distinguishing truth from falsehood by means of judgments based on comparisons. Most important, it serves as a guide to interpreting human behavior by means of judgments that separate signs from the things they signify.

Doubt about how to respond functions as an organizing principle throughout the *Life of Pope*, generating a persistent tendency to oppose appearances and realities, words and deeds, signs and things signified. In discussing the *Essay on Man*, for instance, Johnson colors his narrative by using a visual metaphor which vividly contrasts the poem's innocent and attractive outer appearance with what Johnson sees as its evil inner tendencies: "Its flowers caught the eye which did not see what the gay foliage concealed, and for a time flourished in the sunshine of universal approbation" (3:164). Up to this point, our judgment of Pope and his poem has been complicated by several contrary movements: Pope has been partly cleared of responsibility for the poem's doctrine, since its content has been attributed to Bolingbroke (3:163), and two of its more objectionable lines have been shown to be, at worst, unintentionally sacrilegious (3:162). Yet the metaphor of the appealing but dangerous flower overrides these qualifiers and gives the poem an evil, almost satanic overtone, as though the *Essay on Man* were a forbidden fruit on the tree of knowledge. The essential theme of Johnson's treatment of the *Essay on Man*, the thread that holds together its various polarities, is the theme of seeing and judging clearly, expressed in visual-metaphoric terms: whether or not Bolingbroke intentionally used Pope to undermine Christianity, public debate finally enlightened Pope, who at last had "his eyes open on the side of truth" (3:169).

When Johnson draws such contrasts between appearance and reality, certain epistemological assumptions are at work—namely, that perceptions may be unreliable guides to truth, and that in arriving at the truth one may need to distinguish signs from the things they signify. A good example is the way Johnson refutes Warton's suggestion that the ending of *Windsor Forest* made Addison unhappy, "both as a politician and as a poet. As a politician, because it so highly celebrated that treaty of peace which he deemed so pernicious to the liberties of Europe, and as a poet, because he was deeply conscious that his own *Campaign*, that Gazette in rhyme, contained no strokes of such genuine and sublime poetry as the conclusion before us" (*Lives* 3:106). Johnson's refutation is brief: "The pain that Addison might feel it is not likely that he would confess" (3:106). In a stroke Johnson's dialectic forces the reader to weigh two probabilities by contrasting the sign and the thing signified: it is not entirely improbable that Addison might *feel* distress, but it is very unlikely that he would show any *signs* of it. The underlying structure of this sort of argument may be seen in its epistemological aspect as a logic of probable signs, and in its literary aspect as a logic of decorum. That is, both Lockean probabilism and neoclassical decorum tended to focus attention on the problematic relationship between outward signs and inner states or between behavior and character.[4]

A similar concern with the distinction between appearance and reality is evident in many of Johnson's treatments of specific technical issues such as simile, expressive versification, or the machinery in *The Rape of the Lock*. The argument against the importance of expressive connections between the sound and the sense of verse, for example, is based on a distinction between an apparent resemblance and a real one. Essentially, Johnson argues that our minds lead us to expect correspondences between the sounds of words (signs) and their meanings (things signified) but that our perceptions of such correspondences are often generated merely by our expectations. Johnson conducts his refutation empirically and probabilistically: at one point, anticipating the kind of empiricism that was to be displayed by I. A. Richards, he produces a phonetic approximation of Pope's lines on Sisyphus to show that the sense leads us to imagine expressive effects that are not there or that are faint and insignificant.[5]

Johnson's manner of conducting an evaluative argument involves similar dialectical separations and contrasts. For example, when Johnson focuses on the charge that Pope's Homer "is not Homerical . . . as it wants [Homer's] awful simplicity, his artless grandeur, his unaffected majesty" (3:238), his argumentative strategy is typically contrastive. First he establishes a point of view opposed to his own and concedes that it is partly true, though he does so by using the weakest sort of affirmation, negating a negative ("This cannot totally be denied"). Then he establishes a basis for bridging the gap between this view and his own by seeking the broadest possible grounds for agreement: in the history of mankind, "every age improves in elegance," so that Pope's refinement of Homer's style is justified by historical context (3:239). But this movement from antithesis to synthesis does not clinch the argument. The noun-adjective pairs in Johnson's opening statement were fused antitheses— "simple" yet "awe-inspiring," "grand" yet "artless," "majestic" yet "unaffected"—and Johnson now reanimates these and fuses them in altered form: "Elegance is surely to be desired if it be not gained at the expence of dignity." Johnson caps the argument by humanizing the act of judgment, personifying the poem: "A hero would wish to be loved as well as to be reverenced." This personification complicates the effect of the entire passage, since it adds still more levels of fused implication; its metaphoric equivalences erase the distinctions between writer and poem, between Pope and Homer, between heroic style and heroic behavior, between stylistic decorum and moral decorum, between judging a poem and loving a person. If we stop to analyze the oppositions which Johnson reconciles in this passage, the underlying dialectic appears quite complex, but in a normal reading of this passage, the effect is simple, persuasive, and immediate.

Sometimes Johnson controls the reader's judgment by using satiric contrasts, establishing narrative shifts from sympathetic to objective frames of reference. Johnson establishes satiric perspective in various ways involving contrast: by pointing up situational ironies, by using comic, reductive analogies, by letting shifts of prose style signal shifts of attitude, and by revealing ironic reciprocities in the behaviors of his subjects. Often he uses direct allusions to satiric contexts: Juvenal showed the ironic disproportion between great men's deeds and their ways of dying when he described Hannibal's unheroic death by poisoning; Johnson alludes to Juvenal in noting that Pope died from the effects of "a silver saucepan, in which it was his delight to heat potted lampreys" (3:200).

Similarly, Johnson often generates ironies by juxtaposing private and public frames of reference, as one example has shown. Sometimes he expresses this binary contrast in a phrase—as when he quotes Lady Bolingbroke, who "used to say, in a French phrase, that 'he plaid the politician about cabbages and turnips'" (3:200). (Pope was "un politique aux choux et aux raves," that is, he thought strategically and deliberatively upon trivial subjects.)[6] Johnson pounces on the telling contrast and pairs it with a phrase from one of Young's satires: "He hardly drank tea without a stratagem" (3:200).

Judgment in the
Life of Pope

Sometimes, as in treating Pope's grotto, Johnson devotes a whole passage to such contrasts. He uses a dry, ironic tone to point up the incongruity between a great man's grand accomplishments and his petty amusements: "Here he planted the vines and the quincunx which his verses mention, and being under the necessity of making a subterraneous passage to a garden on the other side of the road he adorned it with fossil bodies, and dignified it with the title of a grotto: a place of silence and retreat, from which he endeavoured to persuade his friends and himself that cares and passions could be excluded" (3:134–35).

By alluding to lines from Pope's Horatian imitation ("know, all the distant Din that World can keep / Rolls o'er my *Grotto*, and but sooths my Sleep" [Pope 17]), Johnson suggests a public context even while introducing private, anecdotal detail; Pope's private whims and public posturings are captured in a single characteristic allusion which takes an added comic twist from Johnson's ironic tone. Johnson also exploits ironic contrasts of diction, letting the fashionable, evocative word "grotto" clash with the dry, precise phrase "subterraneous passage." In a single word, "quincunx," Johnson manages to suggest both the world of gardening and the affectations of the literary man who savors the horticultural obscurities of Sir Thomas Browne's *The Garden of Cyrus*. The contrasting frames of reference are joined by the verb "dignified," which reinforces the crucial point: not Pope's little amusement but precisely the *dignifying* of that amusement makes it foolish.

Johnson's Ciceronian, periodic style helps to reinforce his carefully aimed irony by heightening one's sense that complex, multiple contrasts are being carried out by the syntactical couplings and uncouplings. Johnson's irony in the passage above, for instance, is immediately confirmed and reinforced by the tone and cadence of the unexpected relative clause, phrased like one of Johnson's facetious definitions, which rolls through three contrastive doublets with an increasingly insistent underrhythm, until it breaks like a wave upon a Ciceronian *clausula* in its emphatically foolish closing words: "a *place* of *si*lence and re*treat* from *which* he en*dea*voured to per*suade* his *friends* and him*self* that *cares* and *pas*sions *could be* ex*cluded*." By means of delicately ironic modulations of perspective, counterpointed by shifts of rhythm and tone, Johnson evokes an entire complex of attitudes: once we reach the end of this paragraph on the grotto, we are in the world of the antipastoral, the world of the skeptical city dweller who doubts the notion of pastoral bliss.

One way to describe passages such as this is to say that in them Johnson enforces judgment by placing specific contrasts in general contexts, so that a balance is maintained between levels of generality as well as between tones and attitudes. The grotto is a revealing detail that suggests much about broader topics: Pope's character, his knack for ingenious adaptation, and his strategic approach to life, work, and play. It also enables Johnson to modulate subtly to a genial, comic tonality, accepting yet gently mocking Pope by placing him, first, in the category of the garden-loving English, who more often "need to solicit than exclude the sun," then in the category of "the studious and speculative" whose "amusements seem frivolous and childish," and then in the still more general category of "great men" (3:135). Finally, in a closing shift of perspective, Johnson draws our perception outward to a still more general context that includes the onlookers, ourselves:

> It may be frequently remarked of the studious and speculative that they are proud of their trifles, and that their amusements seem frivolous and childish; whether it be that men conscious of great reputation think themselves above the reach of censure, and safe in the admission of negligent indulgences, or that mankind expect from elevated genius an uniformity of greatness, and

watch its degradation with malicious wonder; like him who having followed with his eye an eagle into the clouds, should lament
that she ever descended to a perch. [3:135]

Johnson encompasses the reader's attitudes in his broad irony:
great men with trivial hobbies seem foolish, but the real folly is to
expect geniuses to maintain unwavering dignity. The foolishness
is compounded by the reading of biographies to learn about great
men's trifles.[7]

Johnson often establishes ironic contrasts by setting in sharp
opposition the two halves of an analogy, so that the triviality of
the tenor is brought out by the contrasting vehicle. For instance,
by dialectically contrasting monetary value with imputed value,
Johnson calls attention to the self-aggrandizing quality in Pope's
"ridiculous and romantick" complaint (in his preface to the Swift-
Pope *Miscellanies*, 1727) that the private papers of sick and dying
authors are frequently plundered "for papers of uncertain and
accidental value . . . as if epigrams and essays were in danger
where gold and diamonds are safe" (3:144, 145). The reductive
effect of that final clause creates some comic momentum which
Johnson immediately exploits in the next sentence, moving to a
still wittier and more outrageous analogy: "A cat hunted for his
musk is, according to Pope's account, but the emblem of a wit
winded by booksellers."

The satiric perspective often generates its opposite. In the instance just quoted, Johnson abruptly reverses himself, as though
the witty analogies have carried him too far; he begins the next
paragraph by sympathetically admitting that Pope had some
grounds for complaint, since during this period a parcel of his
letters was in fact sold and published.

Johnson uses yet another type of satiric contrast when he places
two persons side by side and displays the correspondence or reci-

procity of their respective follies. This sort of side-by-side comparison was encouraged by the generic conventions of the "companion pieces" popular in Johnson's day, ranging from poems in the tradition of "L'Allegro" and "Il Penseroso" to the Hogarth or Rowlandson companion pieces constructed around elaborate arrays of contrasts which must be "read" semiotically like texts.

Here again we can see a connection between a dialectical mode of perception and the epistemological assumptions upon which the mode was based. When a visual artist like Rowlandson showed ironic parallels between, for instance, the respective postures of a country gentleman rising in the early morning and a city gentleman going to bed at the same hour, he was exploiting generic conventions that were built upon a notion of judgment as comparison and contrast (Grego 281–82).

Similarly, when Johnson places writer and patron in mirrored postures of mutual rejection, generic conventions encourage us to perceive ironies through the inherently dialectical process of drawing contrasts and then rising above them:

> These voluntary offers, and this faint acceptance, ended without effect. The patron was not accustomed to such frigid gratitude, and the poet fed his own pride with the dignity of independence. They probably were suspicious of each other. Pope would not dedicate till he saw at what rate his praise was valued; he would be "troublesome out of gratitude, not expectation." Halifax thought himself entitled to confidence; and would give nothing, unless he knew what he should receive. Their commerce had its beginning in hope of praise on one side, and of money on the other, and ended because Pope was less eager of money than Halifax of praise. It is not likely that Halifax had any personal benevolence to Pope; it is evident that Pope looked on Halifax with scorn and hatred. [3:125–26]

Johnson does not overtly say, "Such 'commerce' as this debases both the writer and the patron," but that is one ironic point of the paragraph. The irony is apparent, not through any explicit statement, but through the movement of the prose, which calls attention to its seesaw direction of our attention: "here is the foolish poet, here is the foolish patron."

Johnson works some highly effective variations on this type of satiric contrast. For instance, in discussing the Pope-Addison rivalry, he sets up multiple levels of comparison, using allusion as an economical way of assimilating a present example to a timeless category. In comparing Pope and Addison's rivalry to the rivalry of two Romans, of whom "one could no longer bear an equal, nor the other a superior" (3:128), Johnson not only creates ironic distance by alluding to an ancient parallel but also complicates the irony by means of a second layer of allusion—to Pope's lines on Addison, who could "bear, like the Turk, no brother near the Throne" (Pope 110).

While comparative judgment gives the *Life* its broadest principle of coherence, at another level Johnson's prose style constantly enacts the process of dialectical judgment. In its ingenious syntactical variations, Johnson's prose incessantly dramatizes a process of pausing, weighing alternatives, and then assertively moving forward to a final synthesis: a judgment, a preference, a choice. For instance, in a sentence laden with subordinate comparisons, Johnson comments on Addison's advising Pope not to revise *The Rape of the Lock*: "This has been too hastily considered as an instance of Addison's jealousy; for as he could not guess the conduct of the new design, or the possibilities of pleasure comprised in a fiction of which there had been no examples, he might very reasonably and kindly persuade the author to acquiesce in his own prosperity, and forbear an attempt which he considered as an unnecessary hazard" (3:103). The act of judging

a person's motives involves the weighing of alternative interpretations, and Johnson's syntax enforces the careful qualification of such judgments. But the next sentence is more abrupt:
"Addison's counsel was happily rejected." The sudden contrast in sentence length and sentence structure has the expressive
effect of sweeping away all the considerations conjured up
by Johnson's previous sentence. The overall movement of the
passage, then, is a sort of modulation from judgment to action.
The prose style makes us pause to consider and weigh probable
alternatives but then sweeps us forward abruptly, like life itself.
Whatever Addison's motives might have been, Pope ultimately
had to act by following or rejecting his advice, and whatever our
judgment of Addison's motives may be, Johnson must move on
with the narrative. The contrast in syntax achieves both transitions.

Is this a conscious technique? Here it seems to be, because
Johnson immediately uses it again, as though pleased with the
effect. He ends this paragraph with an image-rich twenty-six-
word sentence describing Pope's imagination at work and then
begins the next paragraph with another short, simple sentence:
"The soft luxuriance of his fancy was already shooting, and all
the gay varieties of diction were ready at his hand to color and
embellish it. His attempt was justified by its success" (3:103–4).
Here, even more strikingly than in the first example, the dialectical contrast in syntax works to express the movement from judgment to action: the first sentence lingeringly evokes the psychological faculty of fancy, while the second abruptly evokes
judgment and its final effect, the completed action.

The effectiveness of his structural use of dialectical contrast is
even more striking if we look not just at syntax but at paragraph
design:

> During this period of his life he was indefatigably diligent, and
> insatiably curious; wanting health for violent, and money for ex-

Judgment in the
Life of Pope

pensive pleasures, and having certainly excited in himself very strong desires of intellectual eminence, he spent much of his time over his books: but he read only to store his mind with facts and images, seizing all that his authors presented with undistinguishing voracity, and with an appetite for knowledge too eager to be nice. In a mind like his, however, all the faculties were at once involuntarily improving. Judgment is forced upon us by experience. He that reads many books must compare one opinion or one style with another; and when he compares, must necessarily distinguish, reject, and prefer. But the account given by himself of his studies was that from fourteen to twenty he read only for amusement, from twenty to twenty-seven for improvement and instruction; that in the first part of this time he desired only to know, and in the second he endeavoured to judge. [3:94]

In this paragraph, dialectical contrasts in diction, syntax, and levels of signification work together not mechanically but organically. In the first sentence, for instance, between Pope's intellectual pleasure and the more worldly pleasure of some young men, the relationship is basically antithetical, but the diction used to describe Pope's hunger for knowledge carries connotations that imply equivalence rather than contrast: "indefatigably," "insatiably," "excited," "strong desires," "seizing," "voracity," and "appetite" all work to suggest the sublimation of Pope's physical hungers into intellectual ones.

Johnson's initial point is that Pope read with the same passionate intensity that a healthier, richer young man might have misspent in gaming, whoring, drinking, and eating, but further antitheses unfold from this first one: the discriminating versus the indiscriminate passion for knowledge and the voluntary versus the involuntary development of judgment. This last distinction is stated only to be erased: judgment may be a faculty governable by the conscious will, Johnson argues, but it improves by unconscious degrees as experience provides it with more materials to work with.

Johnson enforces this last point by using a truncated syllogism whose conclusion is left implied:

> He who reads widely must compare.
> He who compares must judge (distinguish, reject, prefer).
> He who reads widely must judge.

This argument of course cancels out the initial antithetical statement of the paragraph; we have arrived at a point where we can see that *no* intellectual appetite, however voracious, can avoid encouraging some development of the power of discrimination and judgment. This argument, however, is in turn contradicted by the paragraph's final antithetical movement: "But the account given by himself of his studies was that . . . he read . . . first . . . only to know, and . . . second . . . to judge."

These various contrasts all contribute to a larger syntactical design: the paragraph moves from predominantly loose compound sentences to predominantly complex periodic ones, with phrases and clauses marching in tight parallelism, diversified by ellipsis, in the paragraph's final sentence. The overall effect of this shift in syntax is apparent if one contrasts sentences 1 and 5: the first moves forward in a restless fashion that imitates the thing it describes. Its dominant mode is inclusion, as though doublets and parenthetical elements were being acquired and tucked into the sentence spontaneously, as the thought developed. In contrast, the dominant mode of sentence 5 is exclusion: Pope read "*only* for amusement" and "*only* to know." The structure of this final sentence is tight and elliptical, with no parentheses or improvisatory expansions of units; the slightest nuances of diction, such as the subtle antithesis of "desired" and "endeavoured," work to restrict and clarify rather than merely to amplify Johnson's meaning.

Even the cadence of the paragraph works dialectically, by means of the contrast between expanding and contracting movements of syntactical units:

> Sentence 1: 75 words
> Sentence 2: 14 words
> Sentence 3: 7 words
> Sentence 4: 24 words
> Sentence 5: 49 words

Johnson's antithetical style is anything but rigid and predictable; it is rich, various, and beautifully modulated.

Johnson's dialectic exploits the indeterminacy of comparative figures. That is, when Johnson compares Pope's intellectual appetites to the physical appetites of other young men, the reader expects contrast but encounters equivalence. Differences and similarities play against each other expressively because one cannot be sure which is figure and which is ground. In Johnson's great satire *The Vanity of Human Wishes*, mock-epic conventions work to suggest that there is an incongruity between the scales of value appropriate to domestic life and to political life, but Johnson keeps evoking similarities rather than differences. In *The Vanity of Human Wishes*, the reiterated tales of military and political defeat set up powerful and consistent expectations which influence our perception of private life. Johnson applies the language of battle and conspiracy to the social and moral predicaments of a beautiful woman: to overthrow her virtues, "the rival batters, and the lover mines," and she "quits the slipp'ry reign" of social preeminence because no virtues can "defend the pass" against the army of invading vices. In this way Johnson powerfully subverts our optimistic expectations; we hope that domestic life will be relatively free from the discords of political life, but instead we find that some of the horror of military encounter laps over into even the most private of moments: God discerns "the secret *ambush* of a specious pray'r" (see *Complete English Poems* 91, esp. lines 331–54).[8]

In general, the larger the structural components, the more powerful are Johnson's dialectical tendencies. When free to imagine an extended fictional narrative, Johnson tends to impose strong, contrastive patterns such as those of *Rasselas*, where the relationship between sections follows a pattern of dialectical oppositions: the life of emotion and impulse (chap. 17) is followed by the life of total resistance to emotion and impulse (chap. 18); the life of impoverished rusticity (chap. 19) is followed by the life of wealth (chap. 20). Johnson thinks of human motivation in terms of opposed forces of attraction and repulsion, and his bisociative habits of mind result partly from his interest in the problem of choice: "nature sets her gifts on the right hand and on the left" (*Rasselas* 134).

The *Lives of the Poets* is constructed along similar lines; its dramatis personae are often running to something or from something, and their hoped-for escapes (such as pastoral retreat) prove as illusory as their hoped-for goals (such as victory over literary rivals). Johnson's entire way of thinking about human action and motivation may be seen as a pessimistic development of the bisociative moral psychology of Locke, who saw human liberty as inhering in an act of moral judgment—the weighing of a remote versus a proximate reward. Locke "placed the exercise of our liberty in that period of time between desiring and actually determining our wills" (Claudia Johnson 580–81). For Samuel Johnson, this interval can too easily become an interval of moral paralysis. After all, human actions depend upon choice, and well-regulated choice must exist somewhere between the extremes of thoughtless whim and a too thoughtful paralysis of the will. Judgment is the faculty that gives us our moral freedom, and the development of our judgment is the controlling purpose of Johnson's biographical art of contrast.

Assuming that all these dialectical features exist in Johnson's *Life of Pope*, one certainly may still ask whether their presence tells us anything new about Johnson or whether it matters very much. My answer would be that, while Johnson's dialectical tendency has been noticed before, its centrality in his biographical rhetoric has attracted less attention than it deserves. Certainly to Johnson the process of drawing dialectical distinctions between terms was vitally important because he saw it as essential to the very process of generating meaning. What Johnson hated above all was nonsense of the sort that occurs whenever antithetical distinctions are overlooked or whenever a writer engages in a kind of pseudo-antithesis. So when Pope writes of Sir William Trumbull that he was "An honest courtier, yet a patriot too" (3:257), Johnson's comment is brusque and impatient: "There is no opposition between an *honest courtier* and a *patriot*; for an *honest courtier* cannot but be a *patriot*" (3:258). Similarly, when Pope says that in heaven Trumbull "at length enjoys that liberty he lov'd," Johnson comments: "Why should Trumbal [*sic*] be congratulated upon his liberty, who had never known restraint?" (3:258).

Johnson is bothered whenever Pope's use of antithesis seems automatic, as though the poet has temporarily forgotten to control the implications of this pattern of thought. When Pope describes Gay as "in wit, a man; [in] simplicity, a child," Johnson detects the falseness of these antitheses with devastating accuracy: "That Gay was a *man in wit* is a very frigid commendation; to have the wit of a man is not much for a poet. The *wit of man* and the *simplicity of a child* make a poor and vulgar contrast, and raise no ideas of excellence, either intellectual or moral" (3:268–69). When Pope describes Gay as "mild" and "gentle," "temp'ring virtuous rage" with "native humour," Johnson comments sarcastically that "for a man so *mild* and *gentle* to *temper* his *rage* was not difficult" (3:268–69).

Johnson's attacks upon poetic nonsense thus suggest one reason why binary opposition is so pervasive a feature of his style: to fail to draw antithetical distinctions is tantamount to a failure to judge. It is to surrender to unmeaning. This notion of a threat to meaning touches upon some broader functions of binary thinking—global or characterological functions that carry one beyond stylistics, into deconstructive and psychoanalytic readings.

At the broadest level, binary thinking is an expression of a drive to assimilate experience by reducing it to manageable categories. Such thinking strives to reduce the multitude of categories of experience to a few key polarities: good-bad, inner-outer, active-passive, comic-tragic, and so on. Polar thinking reduces as it organizes; but what is remarkable in this context is how *un*-reductive Johnson's habitually polar modes are. Seldom does Johnson's bisociative thinking result in simplistic, either-or kinds of statements.

Psychologically speaking, an important function performed by binary thinking is the coordination and integration of opposed portions of the self. The creative and self-critical aspects of Johnson's identity were always potentially in conflict. His rapid, energetic manner of working, his unwillingness to revise extensively, his unwillingness to look back, are all familiar pieces of evidence suggesting a vigorous resistance to the process of self-doubt. Instead of letting himself be paralyzed by his self-critical tendencies, he turned them into a creative force, a portion of the creative process itself. A dialectical fusing of antithetical terms was for Johnson the ultimate way of placing judgment at the service of the creative impulse.

Eight

Conclusion

Some twenty years ago, after noting that "Johnson's relation to the Enlightenment" has generally been seen as "one of simple opposition," Robert Shackleton suggested how inadequate such a notion really is (76). It is true, he noted, that Johnson was generally on the conservative side of any debate "in relation to which opinions were clearly aligned into the contrasting camps of the *philosophes* and the *anti-philosophes*" (81), yet Johnson shared many points of affinity with the thinkers he predictably opposed: his indebtedness to Locke, his admiration for Bayle and Mandeville, his interest in Feijoo and Sarpi, and even his Diderot-like enthusiasm for the practical and mechanical arts (83–89).

> The situation of Johnson in relation to the Enlightenment is then by no means simple. He believed in the spread of knowledge. He accepted the empiricism of Locke. He leaned to utilitarianism in politics. His natural bent of mind was sceptical. In all these respects he was at one with Voltaire and Diderot. . . . Johnson carried into the second half of the century the outlook, the ideas, and the sympathies of the earliest representatives of the Enlightenment. But to have aligned himself, in the public view or in the

143

light of his own conscience, with the *philosophes* of 1770, atheists
and materialists as they were, would for him have been unthink-
able. [91–92]

Peter Gay, too, using the simultaneity and similarity of *Can-
dide* and *Rasselas* as a takeoff point, finds that in some important
ways Johnson "had the Enlightenment style" (1:21), basing this
observation on his well-documented contention that many of the
"ideas and attitudes generally associated with subversive, athe-
istic philosophers . . . were the common property of most educated men in the eighteenth century" (1:23). In Gay's view, Johnson "detested the philosophes as unprincipled infidels, [but]
accepted much of their program" (1:21). He participated in the
"critical temper" of the age.

Jeffrey Barnouw has taken yet another approach to the problem of assimilating Johnson to the Enlightenment: by focusing on
writers "considered marginal or opposed to the Enlightenment on
the basis of a narrow conception," he writes, "we may arrive at a
more adequate idea of what 'the age' in fact considered enlightenment to be" (190). In trying to arrive at this more adequate conception, Barnouw pairs Johnson with the skeptical philosopher
conspicuously absent from my discussion to this point: David
Hume. If I understand Barnouw correctly, his point is that both
Hume and Johnson exemplify what he calls a "conatist" psychology which stresses "the role of drive, urge, desire as a positive
factor in experience" (192): "Johnson's repeated use of the motto
drawn from the *Aeneid:* 'Possunt quia posse videntur' (which had
already been used in this sense by Bacon) epitomizes the moral
psychology of endeavour which is developed, on a Baconian and
Hobbesian basis, by Johnson—and by other prominent writers of
the Enlightenment including David Hume" (194). To this for-
mulation one might add that, if the Enlightenment mode is characterized by a psychology of human endeavor, such a psychology

further depends upon a psychology of choice, and this is one of Johnson's constant and overriding concerns. The Johnsonian rhetoric which returns again and again to a mode of side-by-side comparison and contrast is a rhetoric designed for the progressive education of human judgment under the influence of experience. Comparative judgments are a model for human choice, hence for human endeavor itself.

As I argued in chapter 3, Johnson seems to have been satisfied by the probabilistic solution to skepticism put forward by the constructive skeptics of the seventeenth century: if we were to withhold belief from all propositions that fall short of certainty, we would be paralyzed and incapable of acting at all. But meanwhile life presses upon us; we must act; and so we have no choice but to act upon the basis of truths merely probable rather than certain, keeping in mind that questions of probability are questions of degrees of assent. In endorsing such a viewpoint, Johnson was "accepting a kind of semi-scepticism and stating it as if it were an answer to scepticism" (Popkin, "Scepticism and Anti-Scepticism" 328), and he was basing his approach upon an epistemological probabilism which uses doubt as a creative "means of assessing and overcoming difficulties" (Chapin, "Common Sense" 62). Doubt leads to comparative judgment, judgment leads to choice, and choice leads to action based upon probable truth. This is Johnson's "conatist" mode as I understand it.

However, it is difficult to prove conclusively the literary influence of an epistemological paradigm. I have been mainly concerned with making a probable case based on an examination of Johnson's creative use of doubt as a means of educating the faculty of judgment; my method has been to place doubt itself in a series of changing contexts—the psychology of doubt, the philosophy of doubt, and the effects of doubt upon Johnson's biographical rhetoric—in order to illustrate the complexity of doubt's manifestations.

The Philosophical
Biographer

But the problems inherent in this sort of argument should be more thoroughly examined before I am done, and illustrations of such problems can be seen if one looks at Johnson's use of the "epistemological doublet." This interesting term was coined by Leo Braudy in his *Narrative Form in History and Fiction:*

> Gibbon's style reflects his belief that any interpretation of the past is at best tentative. Hume attempted to express his balanced and measured view through the order of his periodic sentences. Fielding's typical sentence moves from certainty to contingency through a haze of qualifying clauses. Gibbon's method often seems similar to Fielding's. But his most typical device is a kind of epistemological doublet—"through sincerity or duplicity"—held in unresolved balance by the comprehension of his narrative voice. Gibbon continually asserts in the *Essai* and the *Memoirs* that he believes history-writing necessitates a concern with probabilities rather than certainties. [216]

Here is an interconnection between epistemology and forms of literary expression of precisely the sort I have been pursuing. Braudy clearly believes that the pairing of terms has epistemological origins and derives from the historical period's characteristic concern with probability. Furthermore, as I have noted and as earlier critics have noticed, this sort of ambiguous pairing is a striking feature of Johnson's style as well, so here we seem to have a fairly clear instance of a common epistemological influence upon the literary styles of two writers from the same period.[1]

But Peter Gay sees an entirely different influence at work in Gibbon's use of such doublets—not the probabilism of a post-Lockean sensibility but the insinuating rhetoric of a follower of Tacitus: "Gibbon . . . sees it as his task to penetrate beyond appearances. Hence he can borrow from Tacitus with complete freedom. His sly habit of coupling motives—'conviction or fear,' 'piety or prudence,'—which conveys the ambiguity of action and permits a charitable, while suggesting a cynical, appraisal of human behavior, is pure Tacitus" (1:158).

It is impossible to demonstrate conclusively that this stylistic feature derives solely from a clearly delimited epistemological paradigm or from a single classical precedent. Perhaps one should instead reconcile the two accounts by arguing that, while Gibbon (perhaps Johnson, too) may have borrowed this *feature* from Tacitus, its *function* has shifted for the eighteenth-century writer: it now works not just to suggest a specific, uncharitable interpretation of motives but also to express a broader sense of uncertainty about the entire process by which historical inferences about human motivation are drawn. From this perspective, the "epistemological doublet" can be seen as an example of the way in which the critical temper of the Enlightenment applied classical precedents to the needs of a probabilistic age.

I have already suggested that the transitional character of Johnson's thought derives partly from the shifting character of logic and rhetoric in his period: Aristotelian and post-Lockean logic both have a place in Johnson's thinking, in which the older truth criteria of consistency and consensus coexist with the newer criteria of evidence and experience. As W. S. Howell puts it,

> Neither of these two conceptions has to be rejected if the other is made a principle of scholarship or morality. Nevertheless, the principle of consistency is of maximum use in an age which believes that its major truths have all been discovered, and that its great problem is to establish a consistency between those truths and the rules of conduct. On the other hand, the principle which equates truth with factual accuracy is naturally of first importance in an age of scientific revolution, when old truths are being struck down and new truths established. [*Eighteenth-Century British Logic* 262]

No complete view of Johnson fails to take into account his double allegiances: to traditional rhetoric and to modern; to Aristotle and to Locke; to consistency and to experience; to deduction and to induction; to disputation and to experimentation.

While I have been arguing to this point that Johnson's approach to biography is characterized by a use of doubt as an instrument of inquiry and as a means of educating the reader's judgment, I wish to conclude by suggesting that Johnson's skepticism is an important aspect of his "Enlightenment style" and that it has both ancient and modern affinities. A failure to pay attention to both the old and new aspects of Johnson's use of doubt and skepticism can only distort our perception of him and the period in which he worked.

Thus when Charles Noyes argues that "Johnson had mastered the Humean methodology," he distorts our perception of Johnson (94). Johnson used inverted skeptical arguments to show that the evidences for Christianity are better attested than the evidences showing that the British defeated the French in Canada (Boswell 1:428), and Noyes cites the apparently Humean features of these arguments as evidence that Johnson was a student of Hume's methods. The passage is so thoroughly Humean, Noyes says, that it should be seen as an allusion to, and refutation of, Hume's arguments against miracles: "There was no mention of Hume by name, but the context would make such a mention superfluous" (93). Noyes does not realize that Johnson draws his argument from the arsenal provided by the constructive skeptics of the seventeenth century, who in turn derived their argumentative methods from a tradition of philosophical skepticism reaching back to antiquity (see Walker, "Evidences" 27–41, and chapter 3 of the present book). The error is perpetuated by Donald Siebert, who cites Noyes with approval and sees Johnson as "plac[ing] his arguments in a Humean context" when in fact Johnson is using canons of probability deriving, as Douglas Patey has shown, from ancient sources.[2] I agree that we should take note when Johnson uses Hume-like forms of argument, but we cannot simply assume that "Hume-like" means "Hume-derived," especially when it is important to see that both writers probably derived their techniques from shared sources. Their shared use of doubt as a creative instrument of inquiry, argument, and education is part of the "Enlightenment style" that joins these otherwise disparate writers, and the shared style results from a complex interaction of influences, some ancient, some modern.

The goal of educating the reader's judgment, which Pierre Bayle, the Enlightenment's early spokesman, saw as the primary purpose of criticism, was as modern as the novel and as ancient as the *Nicomachean Ethics*. Aristotle speaks of an ideal "prudent man" in terms that could be taken as describing a man skilled in using his judgment in deciding questions of probable truth:

> For we say that to deliberate well is the most characteristic function of the prudent man; but no one deliberates about things that cannot vary nor yet about variable things that are not a means to some end, and that end a good attainable by action; and a good deliberator in general is a man who can arrive by calculation at the best of the goods attainable by man.
>
> Nor is Prudence a knowledge of general principles only: it must also take account of particular facts, since it is concerned with action, and action deals with particular things. [*Nicomachean Ethics* 345–47]

Here Aristotle is alluding to his own distinction between the dialectical syllogism, which produces probable conclusions, and the apodeictic syllogism, which produces necessary and certain ones. Probability rests upon induction from particular facts rather than upon deductions from general principles, and the purpose of prudential judgment is to provide us with truths sufficiently credible to form a basis for action. In drawing together the concepts of prudential or deliberative judgment, induction, probability, and action, Aristotle at least touched upon ideas that became central to post-Lockean probabilism, although of course Aristotle defined probability in terms of consensus rather than in terms of evidence.

Victoria Kahn sees this Aristotelian doctrine as crucial in determining the relationship between readers and texts during the Renaissance: "The central assumption of the humanist rhetorical tradition is that reading is a form of prudence or of deliberative rhetoric and that a text is valuable insofar as it engages the reader in an activity of discrimination and thereby educates the faculty of practical reason or prudential judgment which is essential to the active life" (11). In a sense, Cicero reinforced Aristotle's influence in moving Renaissance theories of discourse toward an emphasis upon the probable rather than the certain. Cicero's ideal orator approximates the Renaissance conception of the perfectly educated man—undogmatic, able to argue any side of any question, skilled in dialectic, disposed to regard all arguments as essentially probable rather than certain—and the Pyrrhonist skeptic is the man who comes closest to Cicero's ideal orator.

Kahn sees the prudential rhetoric of the Renaissance as gradually reaching a terminal point marked by the skepticism of Hobbes: "At the same time that their texts [i.e., the works of Erasmus, Montaigne, and Hobbes] reveal an awareness of the ideal alliance of rhetoric and prudence, their rhetorical strategies prove to be symptomatic of an increasing anxiety or skepticism about the power of rhetoric to persuade to right action" (27). Thus for Kahn these writers exemplify the decline of prudential rhetoric (27), while I would say rather that this rhetoric was reborn in an altered form. She sees Renaissance humanism as "com[ing] to an end" when prudence was replaced by science as the " 'standard and measure' of political action" (53), with "mathematical certainty . . . [becoming] the standard of reason in politics as well as science" (24), but this seems precisely the reverse of the real case, which was that the seventeenth century initiated an era of creative doubt and concern with probability. The skeptical crisis induced primarily by the Rule of Faith controversy and by the rise of the new science helped to focus attention upon probability and the act of judging probability; it may well have contributed also to the rapid evolution of that highly inductive narrative genre, biography.

Thus I see Johnson, especially Johnson the biographer, as in many ways representing what Peter Gay calls the "critical spirit," an aspect of the Enlightenment that is inherently dialectical in its pursuit of balanced judgment. I see in Johnson's *Lives* a set of subtexts or undercurrents of doubt and uncertainty that links Johnson with key changes that extend through his century. These are empiricism, with its sense of inductive uncertainty; skepticism, with its willingness to suspend judgment; and probabilism, with its sense that there are degrees of assent, and that the crucial test of a proposition is our willingness to act upon it. One final "ism," which I have intentionally postponed until now, is agnosticism, with its questioning of biblical authority. After all, biographies are life writings that acquire meanings by relating the particulars of individual lives to larger patterns of significance, and for Johnson the most inclusive pattern is provided by Christian belief.

If we were to arrange life writings on a spectrum, at one end we would have narratives that make no attempt to assign meaning or value at all, if such a thing were possible. A life of this sort would consist merely of an assortment of dates and facts; the person who is the subject of the life would remain anonymous because no attempt to understand can be made without some framing sense of value and meaning.

At the other end of the spectrum of life writings we could place the Gospel. Here the overall system of meaning totally predominates over the facts of the life related. The events of Jesus' life are seen, not as instances or examples that reveal individual character, but as part of a timeless and eternal system. Whether you read the Gospel typologically or archetypally, the events of Jesus' life acquire significance precisely because they fit into a preordained system of symbolic meaning; what matters is that Jesus' actions fulfilled prophecies, answered needs, and embodied God's will. In a sense, Jesus as an individual man scarcely exists for us; he is an embodiment of God's plan for mankind, and we read the actions of his life as the revelation not of character or individuality but of universal truth.

Somewhere between these two poles—the total suppression of meaning and value, on the one hand, and its total predominance, on the other—lie the varieties of biography as a literary form. Every biography must somehow mediate between the pressures of individual experiences, which are meaningless unless they are assimilated to larger patterns, and the pressures of systems of symbolic meaning, which threaten to overwhelm the stories of individual lives. Only a sacred text can fully assimilate a life story to a system of meaning; only a random assemblage of dates and facts can come close to avoiding the discovery of some meaning and value in the life it recounts.

Empiricism (or a distorted form of empiricism) has been blamed for the eighteenth- and nineteenth-century biographers' tendency to present enormous collections of facts and details without adequate selection or interpretation. Although their works are radically "different in intention, form, and tone, as well as in scope" (Folkenflik, *Samuel Johnson, Biographer* 45), Johnson and Boswell together have been blamed for the naive particularism of later biographers. Richard Schwartz, for instance, has argued that Boswell's "empirical" approach to biography merely "mimics bad science" because it lacks the "systematic shaping" that Johnson gave his biographies (*Boswell's Johnson* 32–33). From this point of view, the putative shortcomings of Boswell and his successors can be seen as having resulted from an empiricism requiring "maximum detail and minimal interpretation" (Nadel 155), while Johnson, with his brevity and selectivity, scarcely seems to be an empiricist at all. Alternatively, Ralph Rader rescues Boswell from the charge of formlessness by arguing that his work is factual yet selective: the *Life of Johnson* is unified by a "grand emotive idea" that holds together the factual details (Vance 29). Boswell's writings thus show "the inherent universality of their subject," while Johnson's "achieve universality of judgment" (Vance 33).

What such arguments about the so-called empiricism of Johnson and Boswell fail to take into account is that both writers are "empirical" in ways more fundamental yet more subtle than any sheer love of facts or anecdotal details. That is, both writers engage the reader's active participation in probabilistically weighing evidence. Johnson fully enacts judgment and constantly seeks closure; Boswell defers judgment and constantly seeks further openings or "expansions" of his subject.[3] But both writers seek a biographical rhetoric that solves the problem of "factuality" versus "artistry" by eliciting the reader's involvement in the process of weighing alternative versions of the truth.

Fredric Bogel suggests that the question of factual truth and its potential opposition to literary artistry has led to all sorts of "oddities of assertion and argument" in discussing Boswell (76), and this observation can be extended to the whole subject of empiricism in biography. What is too often forgotten about biography as a literary form is that it necessarily mediates between the general meaning and the specific instance: the biographer is forced to occupy a middle ground. Confusion results whenever such polarities (factual versus literary, subjective versus objective, neutral versus interpretative) are treated as absolute rather than relative. The totally unselective biography is a mythical beast, as is the totally shaped, interpretative biography. Even the mere chronicler must select and order his material; even the boldly interpretative portraitist is constrained by the image before him. The real opposition is between biographers who, like Johnson, tend to make the process of interpretation visible to the reader and those who, like Boswell, tend to keep it invisible. This is a question less of a literary versus a factual approach than of one type of artistry versus another. Nor is it a question of degrees of empiricism or "domination of fact" (Nadel 5), since Johnson and Boswell together embody complementary aspects of empiricism: its concern with openly evaluating probable inferences (Johnson) and its concern with letting the data seem to speak for themselves (Boswell).

While it cannot be proved that biography as a genre arose in response to the pressures exerted by empirical philosophy, surely the rise of biography resulted at least partly from something broader: the growing secularism and historicism of the age. As scriptural authority was being questioned, and as historicism was suggesting the relativity of human systems of value and belief, biography may have seemed a form ideally suited to the reassertion of pattern and significance in human life. Particularly in Johnson's hands, biography mediated between inductive particulars and the need for larger patterns of meaning. Precept and example animated, or, to use a favorite Johnsonian term, *invigorated*, each other in Johnson's *Lives*.

For both Johnson and Boswell, biographical writing functioned as a way of dealing with a sense of psychological and epistemological uncertainty: "The data of consciousness are evanescent, hard to realize, localize, and grasp—and autobiographical writing—like the parallel emphasis on epistemology so characteristic of post-Cartesian philosophy—became one of the primary literary modes by which uneasy people like Boswell tried to fix and retain past consciousness, and thereby objectify an elusive sense of self" (Kernan 125). In keeping a journal by means of which he eventually constructed a portrait of Johnson, Boswell worked out "a continuing psychological as well as social struggle against chaos, meaninglessness, even nothingness" (Kernan 129), and thus in a sense he refought the same battle that Johnson had waged in his own biographical (and autobiographical) writings.

One reason for Johnson's exemplary status in the history of biography is precisely his openness to doubts about the meaning and value of human lives. The twentieth-century agnostic can find a model and inspiration in this eighteenth-century Christian's biographies, not because of any particular viewpoints he expressed, but because in their totality Johnson's beliefs seem so thoroughly earned. He was the opposite of the unthinking believer. His openness to the difficulties and paradoxes of life attracts the reader, who may not share his religious faith.

One form this openness takes is Johnson's pervasive irony, which has the effect of calling into question, if only to reassert, our sense of providential order. I refer not to rhetorical irony, dramatic irony, the irony of the New Critics, or the ironic mode of Northrop Frye; I am thinking of situational irony, which inheres in a dialectical opposition between human hopes on the one hand and the actual outcome of events on the other. We devoutly hope that the lottery of life will distribute its goods with some semblance of divine justice and order, but irony asserts a kind of cosmic misrule: a charitable man gives a starving author money for a meal; the author buys a roll and chokes to death on it (1:247).

The Philosophical
Biographer

One could argue that, in such ironies, God manifests himself as a trickster and a pretty malicious one at that. I raise this point only to suggest that the notion of God as trickster is part of what Johnson must suppress in maintaining his ironist's stance. For him, situational irony is a kind of prank played upon us but not by a malevolent deity who enjoys the fumblings of the blind and deaf. Rather, the misfiring of worldly expectations is a constant reminder to Johnson—a sign, to use a term common to religion and probabilism—that it is folly to hope for fulfillment in life and that we have recourse to higher goals and higher consolations than any lottery can offer.

Notes

1 · Introduction

1   The concept of "reasonable doubt" in legal proceedings first became important during the period under discussion, and it derived from "sources in some of the philosophical and religious works concerned with the evidence for belief in Christianity which were published during the seventeenth and eighteenth centuries" (Waldman 300).

2   Johnson, *Lives* (3:302, 308), hereafter cited simply by volume and page number unless further identification is needed to avoid confusion.

2 · The "Doubtfulness" of Johnson's *Lives*

1   Scientific tradition linked sight with the intellect more closely than any of the other senses. Johnson's partial blindness suggests another reason why it was natural for him to think of intellectual uncertainty in terms of visual indistinctness. In *The Dynamics of Literary Response*, Norman Holland has linked such imagery with repressed fantasies of the primal scene or experiences of it, but images of visual indistinctness probably gain their power from their ability to represent repressed material generally.

3 · Johnson, Skepticism, and Biography

1   The term "constructive scepticism" is used by Richard H. Popkin, *The History of Scepticism*. See also Popkin's two articles on skepticism

158

Notes

in the eighteenth century. The most helpful discussion of Johnson's skepticism is still that by Robert Voitle; see his 168–80.

2 Philosophical skepticism has traditionally been subdivided into two categories deriving from two Hellenistic schools of philosophy: academic skepticism held "that no knowledge was possible," while Pyrrhonian skepticism held "that there was insufficient and inadequate evidence to determine if any knowledge was possible, and hence that one ought to suspend judgment" (Popkin, *History of Scepticism* xiii).

3 *Language of Learning* 83; as DeMaria notes, it is extreme skepticism's failure "to adjust itself to the various degrees of probation possible" that arouses Johnson's disapproval.

4 See Greene, *Samuel Johnson's Library* 60; see also Johnson, *Lives* 2:33.

5 Barbara Shapiro 14. Johnson finished reading all of Bacon relatively late in life, but he had always admired and imitated Bacon's prose style, and Bacon's influence upon him was lifelong and pervasive; see Boswell 1:219 and 3:194.

6 Like most writers, Schwartz treats Bacon as the representative exponent of the new science and its epistemology. For a contrasting view which places Bacon outside the mainstream of seventeenth-century skeptical epistemology and sees him instead as "essentially of the traditional Aristotelian pattern," see Van Leeuwen 1–12.

7 *Narrative Form* 216. Robert Folkenflik notes Johnson's use of such doublets and cites Braudy on Gibbon in *Samuel Johnson, Biographer* 74–75n9; see also Folkenflik 76–77 on the uncertainties of determining human motives. My entire discussion of Johnson's biographical skepticism attempts to further the points Folkenflik makes in his incisive concluding paragraphs (*Samuel Johnson, Biographer* 216–19).

8 3:206; on Johnson's treatment of letters as biographical evidence, see Folkenflik, *Samuel Johnson, Biographer* 149–57.

9 Folkenflik, *Samuel Johnson, Biographer* 131; see 118–73, esp. 128–31, for a detailed discussion of the entire question of Johnson's interrelation of the literary and the biographical.

4 · Satire and Sympathy in the *Life of Savage*

1 Michael M. Cohen feels that "the Savage biography signals a new tradition—not always in agreement with Johnson's later remarks about biography—which emphasizes the subject's uniqueness, even oddness, and which is not necessarily productive of lessons either cautionary or exemplary" (34). There is some truth to this; Savage is certainly displayed as a unique and eccentric case. But Johnson goes out of his way to draw cautionary and exemplary conclusions from Savage's life story.

2 The tendency I am describing is most pronounced in Edmund Bergler's well-known essay, which discusses Savage's masochistic neurosis with real insight but which irritatingly characterizes Johnson as "naïve" and "not too astute," functioning mainly as an "exceptionally benevolent observer" (62; see also his 54 and 59). For a psychoanalytic view which corrects Bergler's shortcomings, see Gross, "Case History."

3 *Lives* 2:390. For convenience in discussing the *Lives of the Poets*, I use the text of the *Life of Savage* in Hill's edition, but the careful student of this biography will of course want to consult Tracy's edition, as well as the Scolar Press facsimile of the 1748 edition.

4 I find this point confirmed by Robert Uphaus's very similar argument, published in *Studies in Burke and His Time* a year after the first version of this chapter appeared as an article in *Genre*: "The dominant mode both of style and structure in the *Life,*" Uphaus writes, "is one of 'equipoise,' and it is because of this that the reader's initial expectations are so often anticipated and made complicated. For where the reader may be in the habit of seeing things as either/or—that is, reading the *Life* either skeptically or sentimentally—Johnson complicates our reading by continually calling attention to the complementary nature of apparent opposites" (*Impossible Observer* 51). Similarly, Robert Folkenflik sees the *Life* as comprising "a series of brilliant equilibrations" (*Samuel Johnson, Biographer* 197).

5 I cannot bring myself to believe that Johnson's "horror of extramarital intercourse and his championing of marriage and the family as the basis of securing property in society would be sufficient motive for

blackening Lady Macclesfield in this account" (Dussinger, *Discourse* 130). Nor can I accept the notion that "Johnson . . . was not describing a real person at all but a psychic phenomenon" (Gross, "Case History" 41–42). The distinction between a fantasy-mother and a real person may not matter much to some post-Freudian readers, but to Johnson the difference would be a vital one.

6   Alvin Kernan suggests that Johnson's "emotional investment in Savage" prevented him from suspecting that Savage might be an impostor, even while Johnson's discussion of Mrs. Brett "encourages this suspicion" (80).

5 · Johnson's Redaction of Hawkesworth's *Swift*

1   See Victoria Diane Sullivan, "The Biographies of Samuel Johnson" (147–48, 180–84, 201–12). See also Jeffrey Meyers, "Autobiographical Reflections" (37–48).

2   Johnson's general indebtedness to Hawkesworth has long been recognized, but in recent years Paul Korshin has focused attention upon the principal parallels between Johnson's and Hawkesworth's accounts of Swift; see Korshin, "Johnson and Swift" 469–70 n16. John Lawrence Abbott also briefly discusses Johnson's borrowings; see his *John Hawkesworth* (53–56). The *Life of Swift* has been examined more generally in relation to its predecessors by Williams. See also Wayne Warncke, "Samuel Johnson on Swift" (56–64), and Jordan Richman, "Subjectivity" (91–102).

3   Abbott, *John Hawkesworth* 20. See also Abbott's "Dr. Johnson and Dr. Hawkesworth" (2–21).

4   See "Boyle, John," in *The Oxford Companion to English Literature*, 4th ed. (Oxford: Clarendon, 1967). Margaret Drabble has promoted Orrery to "intimate friend of Swift, Pope, and Dr. Johnson" in the fifth edition of the *Companion*.

5   "All in all, Hawkesworth incorporates almost the entirety of Swift's autobiographical fragment, more than 70 items from Deane Swift, about 45 from Delany, and about 20 from Orrery" (Sun 107).

6   3:19. As Irvin Ehrenpreis has noted, Johnson's assessment was

wildly off base: "Perhaps the highest compliment one could pay Swift is the observation that Johnson accepted the pamphlet as operating 'by the mere weight of facts.' . . . For much of the *Conduct* is demonstrably false or misleading" (2:492). Ehrenpreis adds: "A dangerously misleading implication of Johnson's remark is that when Swift does set forth his evidence, he is offering plain facts. Actually, he repeatedly and deliberately errs in both his data and his implications" (2:495).

7   The source of the rumor was Edmond Malone; see George Fisher Russell Barker, "Hawkesworth, John, LL.D.," *Dictionary of National Biography*. But Malone's charge was based on second- and third-hand testimony, as Abbott notes (*John Hawkesworth* 188)—and in any case, Johnson may or may not have heard about it.

6 · The Probable and the Marvelous in the *Life of Milton*

1   For a survey of such responses to Johnson's criticism of *Lycidas*, see Fleischauer 235–38.

2   Of course, inductive truth criteria were not new in any absolute sense; rather, they assumed a new relative centrality when the "rejection of the principle of authority" was reinforced by a new emphasis "on evidence rather than the rhetorical skill of the writer" (Barbara Shapiro 229–30).

3   According to Patey, "this interpretation of probability remains central through the seventeenth century" (4).

4   Johnson was also in a sense at the mercy of the language. In writing about Johnson, I too am sometimes forced to use "marvelous" and "probable" as antithetical terms.

5   See Patey, esp. 147–66.

6   Bell 127. As Robert Folkenflik has noted, Johnson was especially careful to distinguish between life and art, so that the heroic qualities of Milton's art should not blind us to some of the less than heroic aspects of his life. See *Samuel Johnson, Biographer* 125, 136–37.

7   Lawrence Lipking has observed that, while "we expect to learn what the egotistic rebel shares with the great poet . . . , Johnson never

explicitly satisfies that expectation." However, Lipking argues, Johnson establishes enough lines of implicit connection between the biographical and critical sections to create "an impression of Milton that is indivisible" (*Ordering of the Arts* 438).

8   Oliver F. Sigworth, "Johnson's *Lycidas*" 161; Fleischauer 246. Johnson's phrasing ("inherent improbability") makes it hard to accept Victor J. Milne's argument that "the criticism [of *Lycidas*] is not levelled at the whole genre of pastoral but merely at the unfortunate combination of the pastoral with inappropriate subject matter." It is true, however, that, in *Rambler* 37, Johnson "censured the pastoral elegy by appealing to a criterion of dramatic consistency—a part of that broad Renaissance concept of *decorum*" (Milne 301).

9   "Samuel Johnson and Reader-Response Criticism" 98. See also Damrosch's *Johnson's Criticism* 79–92, where he argues that "the deepest lesson of Johnson's criticism of pastoral is that he hated the restrictions of arbitrary theory, especially when used to underwrite a moribund genre, and was prepared to rethink its theoretical basis in ways that point forward rather than back" (92).

10   Weinbrot 407. See also Bell 128–29.

7 · Judgment and the Art of Contrast in the *Life of Pope*

1   See "Judgment," Samuel Johnson, *A Dictionary*. As Robert De-Maria observes, "judgment has to do with the large area of probability and relative value, and it leaves reason in command of truth and moral certainty" (*Language of Learning* 99).

2   See Hagstrum, *Samuel Johnson's Literary Criticism* 153–72.

3   Robert DeMaria argues in detail that Johnson's criticism "relies upon the expectation and the convention that critical terms appear in opposing pairs" ("Johnson's Form of Evaluation" 506).

4   See Patey, esp. 87ff.

5   Richards constructs a similar phonetic "dummy" in discussing poetic meter; see *Practical Criticism* 220.

6   The contrastive pairing of gardening and politics was a com-

monplace at least as ancient as the story of Cincinnatus; one thinks of Marvell's Cromwell in his "private Gardens, where / He liv'd reserved and austere, / As if his highest plot / To plant the Bergamot" (Marvell 87). The gardening/politics pairing was of course especially appropriate to Pope.

7 On Johnson's satiric use of anecdotal material, see Folkenflik, *Samuel Johnson, Biographer* 49–51.

8 Folkenflik has carefully described the influence of heroic and mock-heroic conventions in the *Lives*; see his *Samuel Johnson, Biographer* 56–70, esp. 63.

8 · Conclusion

1 Robert Folkenflik draws attention to Johnson's use of such doublets and cites Braudy on Gibbon in *Samuel Johnson, Biographer* 74–75n9.

2 Siebert, "Johnson and Hume" 545; on ancient canons of evidence, see Patey 35–74.

3 On Boswell's use of expansive, metonymic structure, see Nadel 164–68.

Bibliography

Abbott, John L[awrence]. "Dr. Johnson and Dr. Hawkesworth: A Literary Friendship." *New Rambler* ser. C 111 (1971):2–21.

———. *John Hawkesworth: Eighteenth-Century Man of Letters.* Madison: U of Wisconsin P, 1982.

Addison, Joseph. *The Spectator.* Ed. Donald F. Bond. 5 vols. Oxford: Clarendon, 1965.

Alkon, Paul K[ent]. "The Intention and Reception of Johnson's *Life of Savage.*" *Modern Philology* 72 (1974):139–50.

———. "Johnson's Conception of Admiration." *Philological Quarterly* 48 (1969):59–81.

———. *Samuel Johnson and Moral Discipline.* [Evanston, IL]: Northwestern UP, 1967.

Allen, Don Cameron. *Doubt's Boundless Sea: Skepticism and Faith in the Renaissance.* Baltimore: Johns Hopkins UP, 1964.

Allison, James. "Joseph Warton's Reply to Dr. Johnson's *Lives.*" *Journal of English and Germanic Philology* 51 (1952):186–91.

Altick, Richard D. *Lives and Letters: A History of Literary Biography in England and America.* New York: Knopf, 1965.

Aristotle. *The Nicomachean Ethics.* Trans. H. Rackham. Rev. ed. Loeb Classical Library. Cambridge: Harvard UP, 1934.

Barnouw, Jeffrey. "Johnson and Hume Considered as the Core of a New 'Period Concept' of the Enlightenment." *Studies on Voltaire and the Eighteenth Century* 190 (1980):189–96.

Bate, W[alter] Jackson. Introduction. *Essays from the "Rambler," "Adventurer," and "Idler."* New Haven: Yale UP, 1968. xi–xxix.

————. "Johnson and Satire Manqué." Bond 145–60.

————. *Samuel Johnson*. 1977. New York: Harvest-Harcourt, 1979.

Batten, Charles L., Jr. "Samuel Johnson's Sources for 'The Life of Roscommon.'" *Modern Philology* 72 (1974):185–89.

Battersby, James L. "John Nichols on a Johnson Letter." *Studies in Bibliography* 23 (1970):179–83.

————. "Johnson and Shiels: Biographers of Addison." *Studies in English Literature* 9 (1969):521–37.

————. "Patterns of Significant Action in 'The Life of Addison.'" *Genre* 2 (1969):28–42.

————. *Rational Praise and Natural Lamentation: Johnson, "Lycidas," and Principles of Criticism*. Rutherford, NJ: Fairleigh Dickinson UP, 1980.

————. "Samuel Johnson's 'Life of Addison': Sources, Composition, and Structure." 2 vols. Diss. Cornell U, 1965.

Becker, Ernest. *The Denial of Death*. New York: Free, 1975.

Bell, Vereen M. "Johnson's Milton Criticism in Context." *English Studies* 49 (1968):127–32.

Bergler, Edmund. "Samuel Johnson's 'Life of the Poet Richard Savage'— A Paradigm for a Type." *American Imago* 4.4 (1947):42–63.

Berland, K. J. H. "Johnson's Life-Writing and the *Life of Dryden*." *Eighteenth Century: Theory and Interpretation* 23 (1982):197–218.

Berwick, Donald. *The Reputation of Jonathan Swift, 1781–1882*. 1941. New York: Haskell, 1965.

Bogel, Fredric V. "'Did you once see Johnson plain?': Reflections on Boswell's *Life* and the State of Eighteenth-Century Studies." Vance 73–93.

Bond, W. H., ed. *Eighteenth-Century Studies in Honor of Donald F. Hyde*. New York: Grolier Club, 1970.

Booth, Mark W. "Johnson's Critical Judgments in the *Lives of the Poets*." *Studies in English Literature* 16 (1976):505–15.

————. "Proportion and Value in Johnson's *Lives of the Poets*." *South Atlantic Bulletin* 43.1 (1978):49–57.

Boswell, James. *Boswell's Life of Johnson*. Ed. George Birkbeck Hill and L. F. Powell. 6 vols. Oxford: Clarendon, 1934–50.

Bowyer, William. *Miscellaneous Tracts*. London: 1785.

Boyce, Benjamin. "Johnson's *Life of Savage* and Its Literary Background." *Studies in Philology* 53 (1956):576–98.

———. "Samuel Johnson's Criticism of Pope in the *Life of Pope*." *Review of English Studies* n.s. 5 (1954):37–46.

Boyle, John, fifth earl of Orrery. *Remarks on the Life and Writings of Jonathan Swift*. London: 1752.

Brady, Frank, ed. *Literary Theory and Structure: Essays in Honor of William K. Wimsatt*. New Haven: Yale UP, 1973.

———. "The Strategies of Biography and Some Eighteenth-Century Examples." Brady, *Literary Theory and Structure* 245–65.

Braudy, Leo. "Lexicography and Biography in the *Preface* to Johnson's *Dictionary*." *Studies in English Literature* 10 (1970):551–56.

———. *Narrative Form in History and Fiction: Hume, Fielding, and Gibbon*. Princeton: Princeton UP, 1970.

Bredvold, Louis I. *The Intellectual Milieu of John Dryden*. University of Michigan Publications 12. 1934. Ann Arbor: Ann Arbor Paperbacks–U of Michigan P, 1956.

Brink, J[eanie] R. "Johnson and Milton." *Studies in English Literature* 20 (1980):493–503.

Bronson, Bertrand H. *Johnson Agonistes and Other Essays*. Berkeley: U of California P, 1965.

———. "A Note on the *Life of Savage*." *Samuel Johnson: "Rasselas," Poems, and Selected Prose*. Ed. B. H. Bronson. 3rd ed. San Francisco: Rinehart, 1971. xxi–xxviii.

———. Introduction. *Samuel Johnson: "Rasselas," Poems, and Selected Prose*. Ed. B. H. Bronson. 3rd ed. San Francisco: Rinehart, 1971. xi–xx.

Brown, Stuart Gerry. "Dr. Johnson and the Religious Problem." *English Studies* 20 (1938):1–17.

Browning, John D[udley], ed. *Biography in the Eighteenth Century*. Publications of the McMaster University Association for Eighteenth-Century Studies 8. New York: Garland, 1980.

Brownley, Martine Watson. "Johnson's *Lives of the English Poets* and Earlier Traditions of the Character Sketch in England." Engell 29–53.

168

Bibliography

Brush, Craig. *Montaigne and Bayle: Variations on the Theme of Skepticism*. International Archives of the History of Ideas 14. The Hague: Martinus Nijhoff, 1966.

Burke, John J., Jr. "Excellence in Biography: *Rambler* 60 and Johnson's Early Biographies." *South Atlantic Bulletin* 44.2 (1979):14–34.

Bury, R. G. Introduction. *Outlines of Pyrrhonism*. By Sextus Empiricus. Trans. R. G. Bury. Loeb Classical Library. Cambridge: Harvard UP, 1933.

Byrd, Max. "Johnson's Spiritual Anxiety." *Modern Philology* 78.4 (1981): 38–78.

Campbell, Hilbert H. "Shiels and Johnson: Biographers of Thomson." *Studies in English Literature* 12 (1972):535–44.

Carroll, Richard Allen. "Johnson's *Lives of the Poets* and Currents of English Criticism, 1750–1779." Diss. U of Michigan, 1950.

Carver, George. *Alms for Oblivion: Books, Men, and Biography*. Milwaukee: Bruce, 1946. 123–36.

Chapin, Chester. "Johnson and Pascal." Middendorf, *English Writers* 3–16.

———. *The Religious Thought of Samuel Johnson*. Ann Arbor: U of Michigan P, 1968.

———. "Samuel Johnson and the Scottish Common Sense School." *The Eighteenth Century: Theory and Interpretation* 20 (1979):50–64.

Cicero. *De oratore*. Trans. E. W. Sutton and H. Rackham. Loeb Classical Library. 2 vols. Cambridge: Harvard UP, 1942.

Clifford, James L. *Young Sam Johnson*. 1955. New York: Hesperides-McGraw, 1961.

Clifford, James L., and Donald J. Greene. *Samuel Johnson: A Survey and Bibliography of Critical Studies*. Minneapolis: U of Minnesota P, 1970.

Cockshut, A. O. J. *Truth to Life: The Art of Biography in the Nineteenth Century*. New York: Harcourt, 1974.

Cohen, Michael M. "The Enchained Heart and the Puzzled Biographer: Johnson's *Life of Savage*." *New Rambler* ser. C 118 (1977):33–40.

Cox, Stephen D. *"The Stranger within Thee": Concepts of the Self in Late-Eighteenth-Century Literature*. Pittsburgh: U of Pittsburgh P, 1980.

Curley, E. M. *Descartes against the Skeptics*. Cambridge: Harvard UP, 1978.

Daghlian, Philip B., ed. *Essays in Eighteenth-Century Biography*. Bloomington: Indiana UP, 1968.

Damrosch, Leopold, Jr. "Samuel Johnson and Reader-Response Criticism." *The Eighteenth Century: Theory and Interpretation* 21 (1980): 91–108.

——. *Samuel Johnson and the Tragic Sense*. Princeton: Princeton UP, 1972.

——. *The Uses of Johnson's Criticism*. Charlottesville: UP of Virginia, 1976.

Darbishire, Helen. *The Early Lives of Milton*. 1932. New York: Barnes, 1965.

——. *Milton's* Paradise Lost. 1951. Folcroft, PA: Folcroft, 1969.

Davidson, Virginia Spencer. "Johnson's *Life of Savage*: The Transformation of a Genre." *Studies in Biography*. Ed. Daniel Aaron. Harvard English Studies 8. Cambridge: Harvard UP, 1978. 57–72.

Delany, Patrick. *Observations upon Lord Orrery's Remarks on the Life and Writings of Dr. Jonathan Swift*. London: 1754.

DeMaria, Robert, Jr. *Johnson's "Dictionary" and the Language of Learning*. Chapel Hill: U of North Carolina P, 1986.

——. "Johnson's Form of Evaluation." *Studies in English Literature* 19 (1979):501–14.

Dodsley, Robert. *The Preceptor*. 2 vols. London: 1748.

Drabble, Margaret, comp. and ed. *The Oxford Companion to English Literature*. 5th ed. 1985.

Dussinger, John A. *The Discourse of the Mind in Eighteenth-Century Fiction*. Studies in English Literature 80. The Hague: Mouton, 1974.

——. "Style and Intention in Johnson's *Life of Savage*." *ELH* 37 (1970):564–80.

Edinger, William. *Samuel Johnson and Poetic Style*. Chicago: U of Chicago P, 1977.

Ehrenpreis, Irvin. *Swift: The Man, His Works, and the Age*. 3 vols. Cambridge: Harvard UP, 1962–83.

Ellis, Frank H. "Johnson and Savage: Two Failed Tragedies and a Failed

Tragic Hero." *The Author in His Work: Essays on a Problem in Criticism.* Ed. Louis L[ohr] Martz and Aubrey Williams. New Haven: Yale UP, 1978. 337–46.

Engell, James, ed. *Johnson and His Age.* Harvard English Studies 12. Cambridge: Harvard UP, 1984.

Evans, Bergan B. "Dr. Johnson as a Biographer." Diss. Harvard U, 1932.

———. "Dr. Johnson's Theory of Biography." *Review of English Studies* 10 (1934):301–10.

Ferreira, M. Jamie. *Scepticism and Reasonable Doubt: The British Naturalist Tradition in Wilkins, Hume, Reid, and Newman.* Oxford: Oxford UP, 1987.

Fix, Stephen. "Distant Genius: Johnson and the Art of Milton's Life." *Modern Philology* 81 (1984):244–64.

———. "A Parable of Talents: Samuel Johnson's Criticism of Milton." Diss. Cornell U, 1980.

Fleeman, J. D. "The Making of Johnson's *Life of Savage*, 1744." *Library* 5th ser. 22 (1967):346–52.

———, ed. *The Sale Catalogue of Samuel Johnson's Library.* English Literary Studies Monograph Series 2. Victoria, BC: U of Victoria, 1975.

———. "Some Proofs of Johnson's *Prefaces to the Poets*." *Library.* 5th ser. 17 (1962):213–30.

Fleischauer, Warren. "Johnson, *Lycidas*, and the Norms of Criticism." Wahba 235–56.

Fogle, Richard Harter. "Johnson and Coleridge on Milton." *Bucknell Review* 14 (1966):26–32.

Folkenflik, Robert. "Johnson's Art of Anecdote." *Racism in the Eighteenth Century.* Ed. Harold E. Pagliaro. Studies in Eighteenth-Century Culture 3. Cleveland: P of Case Western Reserve U, 1973. 171–81.

———. "Pope and Johnson's *Life of Savage*." *Notes and Queries* 20 (1973): 211–12.

———. "Samuel Johnson as Biographer." Diss. Cornell U, 1968.

———. *Samuel Johnson, Biographer.* Ithaca: Cornell UP, 1978.

Fussell, Paul. *Samuel Johnson and the Life of Writing*. New York: Harcourt, 1971.

Gay, Peter. *The Enlightenment: An Interpretation*. 2 vols. New York: Knopf, 1966–69.

Grange, Kathleen M. "Samuel Johnson's Account of Certain Psychoanalytic Concepts." *Journal of Nervous and Mental Disease* 135 (1962): 93–98.

Greene, Donald. *The Politics of Samuel Johnson*. New Haven: Yale UP, 1960.

———. "Response to Mr. Stanlis's Comment." *Journal of British Studies* 2.2 (1963):84–87.

———. *Samuel Johnson*. Twayne English Authors Series 95. New York: Twayne, 1970.

———. "Samuel Johnson." *The Craft of Literary Biography*. Ed. Jeffrey Meyers. New York: Schocken, 1985. 9–32.

———. *Samuel Johnson: A Collection of Critical Essays*. Englewood Cliffs: Prentice, 1965.

———. "Samuel Johnson and 'Natural Law.'" *Journal of British Studies* 2.2 (1963):59–75.

———. *Samuel Johnson's Library: An Annotated Guide*. English Literary Studies Monograph Series 1. Victoria, BC: U of Victoria, 1975.

Grego, Joseph. *Rowlandson the Caricaturist*. 2 vols. 1880. New York: Collector's Editions, 1970.

Gross, Gloria Sybil. "Johnson on Psychopathology." Korshin and Allen 271–87.

———. "Samuel Johnson's Case History of Richard Savage." *University of Hartford Studies in Literature* 12 (1980):39–47.

Grundy, Isobel. "Samuel Johnson: A Writer of Lives Looks at Death." *Modern Language Review* 79 (1984):257–65.

———, ed. *Samuel Johnson: New Critical Essays*. Totowa: Vision-Barnes, 1984.

Hacking, Ian. *The Emergence of Probability: A Philosophical Study of Early Ideas about Possibility, Induction, and Statistical Inference*. London: Cambridge UP, 1975.

172

Bibliography

Hagstrum, Jean H. "Johnson and the *Concordia Discors* of Human Relationships." *The Unknown Samuel Johnson.* Ed. John J. Burke, Jr., and Donald Kay. Madison: U of Wisconsin P, 1983. 39–53.

———. "The Nature of Dr. Johnson's Rationalism." *ELH* 17 (1950): 191–205.

———. *Samuel Johnson's Literary Criticism.* 1952. Chicago: U of Chicago P, 1967.

Halsband, Robert. "The 'Penury of English Biography' before Samuel Johnson." Browning 112–27.

Hanchock, Paul. "The Structure of Johnson's *Lives:* A Possible Source." *Modern Philology* 74 (1976):75–77.

Hansen, Marlene R. "*Rasselas,* Milton, and Humanism." *English Studies* 60 (1979):14–22.

Hardy, John P. "An Echo of Addison on Lee in Johnson on Thomson." *Notes and Queries* 30 (1983):53–54.

———. Introduction. *Johnson's "Lives of the Poets": A Selection.* Oxford Paperback English Texts. Oxford: Clarendon, 1971. vii–xv.

———. *Samuel Johnson: A Critical Study.* London: Routledge, 1979.

———. "Stockdale's Defence of Pope." *Review of English Studies* n.s. 18 (1967):49–54.

Harth, Phillip. *Contexts of Dryden's Thought.* Chicago: U of Chicago P, 1968.

Havens, Raymond Dexter. *The Influence of Milton on English Poetry.* Cambridge: Harvard UP, 1922.

Hawkesworth, John. "An Account of the Life of the Reverend Jonathan Swift." *The Works of Jonathan Swift.* Ed. John Hawkesworth. 12 vols. [large 8vo]. London: 1754–55. 1:1–76.

Hill, George Birkbeck, ed. *Johnsonian Miscellanies.* 2 vols. 1897. New York: Barnes, 1966.

Hilles, Frederick W[hiley]. "Dr. Johnson on Swift's Last Years: Some Misconceptions and Distortions." *Philological Quarterly* 54 (1975): 370–79.

———. *Johnson on Dr. Arbuthnot.* New Haven: Privately printed for The Johnsonians [George Grady P], 1957.

————. "The Making of *The Life of Pope.*" *New Light on Dr. Johnson.* Ed. Frederick W[hiley] Hilles. New Haven: Yale UP, 1959. 257–84.

Holland, Norman. *The Dynamics of Literary Response.* Oxford: Oxford UP, 1968.

Honan, Park. "Dr. Johnson and Biography." *Contemporary Review* (London) 245 (1984):304–10.

Horne, Colin J. "The Biter Bit: Johnson's Strictures on Pope." *Review of English Studies* n.s. 27 (1976):310–13.

Howell, Wilbur Samuel. *Eighteenth-Century British Logic and Rhetoric.* Princeton: Princeton UP, 1971.

————. *Logic and Rhetoric in England, 1500–1700.* 1956. New York: Russell, 1961.

Irwin, George. *Samuel Johnson: A Personality in Conflict.* N.p.: Auckland UP; Oxford: Oxford UP, 1971.

Johnson, Claudia. "Samuel Johnson's Moral Psychology and Locke's 'Of Power.'" *Studies in English Literature* 24 (1984):563–82.

Johnson, Maurice. "A Literary Chestnut: Dryden's 'Cousin Swift.'" *PMLA* 67 (1952):1024–34.

Johnson, Oliver A. *Skepticism and Cognitivism: A Study in the Foundations of Knowledge.* Berkeley: U of California P, 1978.

Johnson, Samuel. *An Account of the Life of Mr. Richard Savage, Son of the Earl Rivers.* 1748; rpt. Menston, Eng.: Scolar, 1971.

————. *The Complete English Poems.* Ed. J. D. Fleeman. 1971. New York: St. Martin's, 1974.

————. *A Dictionary of the English Language.* 1755. New York: Arno, 1979.

————. *Early Biographical Writings of Dr. Johnson.* Ed. J. D. Fleeman. Farnborough, Eng.: Gregg, 1973.

————. *The Letters of Samuel Johnson.* Ed. R. W. Chapman. 3 vols. Oxford: Clarendon, 1952.

————. *Life of Savage.* Ed. Clarence Tracy. Oxford: Clarendon, 1971.

————. *Lives of the English Poets.* Ed. George Birkbeck Hill. 3 vols. Oxford: Clarendon, 1905.

——. *The Poems of Samuel Johnson.* Ed. David Nichol Smith and Edward L. McAdam. Oxford: Clarendon, 1941.

——. *Works.* 11 vols. London: Talboys and Wheeler, 1825.

——. *The Works of the English Poets, with Prefaces, Biographical and Critical, by Samuel Johnson.* London: 1779–81.

——. *The Yale Edition of the Works of Samuel Johnson.* New Haven: Yale UP, 1958–.

Kahn, Victoria. *Rhetoric, Prudence, and Skepticism in the Renaissance.* Ithaca: Cornell UP, 1985.

Keast, William R. "Johnson and 'Cibber's' *Lives of the Poets,* 1753." *Restoration and Eighteenth-Century Literature.* Ed. Carroll Camden. Chicago: U of Chicago P for Rice U, 1963. 89–101.

——. "Samuel Johnson and Thomas Maurice." Bond 63–79.

Kenshur, Oscar. *Open Form and the Shape of Ideas: Literary Structures as Representations of Philosophical Concepts in the Seventeenth and Eighteenth Centuries.* Lewisburg, PA: Bucknell UP, 1986.

Kernan, Alvin. *Printing Technology, Letters, and Samuel Johnson.* Princeton: Princeton UP, 1987.

Kirkley, Harriet. "Johnson's *Life of Pope:* Fact as Fiction." *Wascana Review* 15.2 (1980):69–80.

Knickerbocker, James Harris. "Swift Expires: Johnson's *Life of Swift* as Moral Exemplum and Psychological Study." Diss. Washington State U, 1975.

Korshin, Paul J. "Johnson and the Earl of Orrery." Bond 29–43.

——. "Johnson's Conception of Admiration." *Philological Quarterly* 48 (1969):59–81.

——. "Samuel Johnson and Swift: A Study in the Genesis of Literary Opinion." *Philological Quarterly* 48 (1969):464–78.

Korshin, Paul J., and Robert R. Allen, eds. *Greene Centennial Studies: Essays Presented to Donald Greene in the Centennial Year of the University of Southern California.* Charlottesville: U of Virginia P, 1984.

Krutch, Joseph Wood. *Samuel Johnson.* New York: Holt, 1944.

Lam, George Lorant. "Johnson's Lives of the Poets: Their Origin, Text, and History, with Remarks on Sources and Comments on His Life of Cowley." Diss. Cornell U, 1938.

Lipking, Lawrence. "Johnson and the Meaning of Life." Engell 1–27.

———. *The Ordering of the Arts in Eighteenth-Century England.* Princeton: Princeton UP, 1970.

Locke, John. *An Essay concerning Human Understanding.* Ed. Peter H. Nidditch. Oxford: Clarendon, 1975.

Longaker, Mark. *English Biography in the Eighteenth Century.* 1931. New York: Octagon, 1971.

Lynn, Steven. "Johnson's *Rambler* and Eighteenth-Century Rhetoric." *Eighteenth-Century Studies* 19 (1986):461–79.

McAdam, E. L., Jr. *Dr. Johnson and the English Law.* Syracuse: Syracuse UP, 1951.

McCarthy, William. "The Composition of Johnson's *Lives:* A Calendar." *Philological Quarterly* 60 (1981):53–67.

———. "The Moral Art of Johnson's *Lives.*" *Studies in English Literature* 17 (1977):503–17.

McGilchrist, Iain. *Against Criticism.* London: Faber, 1982.

Marvell, Andrew. *The Poems and Letters of Andrew Marvell.* Ed. H. M. Margoliouth. 2 vols. 2nd ed. Oxford: Clarendon, 1952.

Mast, Daniel Dee. "Philosophical Speculatists: Representatives of the Age of Enlightenment." *Enlightenment Essays* 2 (1971):23–29.

Meyers, Jeffrey. "Autobiographical Reflections in Johnson's 'Life of Swift.'" *Discourse* [Concordia College] 8 (1965):37–48.

Middendorf, John H[arlan], ed. *English Writers of the Eighteenth Century.* New York: Columbia UP, 1971.

———. "Ideas vs. Words: Johnson, Locke, and the Edition of Shakespeare." Middendorf, *English Writers* 249–72.

———. "Johnson as Editor: Some Proofs of the 'Prefaces.'" Bond 89–106.

Milne, Victor J. "Johnson's Continuity with the Renaissance Critical Tradition." *Eighteenth-Century Studies* 2 (1969):300–1.

Nadel, Ira Bruce. *Biography: Fiction, Fact, and Form.* New York: St. Martin's, 1984.

Nielsen, Kai. *Scepticism*. New Studies in the Philosophy of Religion. London: Macmillan; New York: St. Martin's, 1973.

Noxon, James. "Human Nature: General Theory and Individual Lives." Browning 8–27.

Noyes, Charles E. "Samuel Johnson, Student of Hume." *University of Mississippi Studies in English* 3 (1962):91–94.

Nuttall, A. D. *A Common Sky: Philosophy and the Literary Imagination*. Berkeley: U of California P, 1974.

On the Lives of the Poets (1781–1782). New York: Garland, 1975.

Osborn, James M. "Samuel Johnson." *John Dryden: Some Biographical Facts and Problems*. 1940. Rev. ed. Gainesville: U of Florida P, 1965. 22–38.

Osler, Margaret J. "Certainty, Scepticism, and Scientific Optimism: The Roots of Eighteenth-Century Attitudes Toward Scientific Knowledge." *Probability, Time, and Space in Eighteenth-Century Literature*. Ed. Paula R. Backscheider. New York: AMS, 1979. 3–28.

Patey, Douglas Lane. *Probability and Literary Form: Philosophic Theory and Literary Practice in the Augustan Age*. Cambridge: Cambridge UP, 1984.

Pettit, Henry. "The Making of Croft's Life of Young for Johnson's *Lives of the Poets*." *Philological Quarterly* 54 (1975):333–41.

Phillips, Steven R. "Johnson's *Lives of the English Poets* in the Nineteenth Century." *Research Studies* (Washington State U) 39 (1975):175–90.

Pierce, Charles E., Jr. "The Conflict of Faith and Fear in Johnson's Moral Writing." *Eighteenth-Century Studies* 15 (1982):317–38.

———. *The Religious Life of Samuel Johnson*. Hamden: Archon-Shoe String, 1983.

Pope, Alexander. *Imitations of Horace with an Epistle to Dr. Arbuthnot and the Epilogue to the Satires*. Vol. 4 (2nd ed. rev.) of *The Twickenham Edition of the Poems of Alexander Pope*. Ed. John Butt et al. 11 vols. London: Methuen, 1938–68.

Popkin, Richard H. *The History of Scepticism from Erasmus to Spinoza*. 1960. Rev. ed. 1964. Berkeley: U of California P, 1979.

———. Preface. *The Problem of Certainty in English Thought, 1630–1690*. By Henry G. Van Leeuwen. International Archives of the History of Ideas 3. 2nd ed. The Hague: Martinus Nijhoff, 1970. i–xii.

————. "Scepticism and Anti-Scepticism in the Latter Part of the Eighteenth Century." *Woman in the Eighteenth Century and Other Essays.* Ed. Paul Samuel Fritz and Richard Morton. Publications of the McMaster University Association for Eighteenth Century Studies 4. Toronto: Hakkert, 1976. 319–43.

————. "Scepticism in the Enlightenment." *Studies on Voltaire and the Eighteenth Century* 26 (1963):1321–45.

Potter, Robert. *An Inquiry into Some Passages in Dr. Johnson's "Lives of the Poets": Particularly His Observations on Lyric Poetry, and the Odes of Gray.* 1783. New York: Garland, 1971.

Quinlan, Maurice. *Samuel Johnson: A Layman's Religion.* Madison: U of Wisconsin P, 1964.

Rader, Ralph W. "Literary Form in Factual Narrative: The Example of Boswell's *Johnson*." Daghlian 3–42. Rpt. in Vance 25–52.

Raleigh, Sir Walter Alexander. *Six Essays on Johnson.* 1910. New York: Russell, 1965.

Reichard, Hugo M. "Boswell's Johnson, the Hero Made by a Committee." *PMLA* 95 (1980):225–33.

Rescher, Nicholas. *Scepticism: A Critical Reappraisal.* Totowa: Rowman, 1980.

Rhodes, Rodman D. "*Idler* No. 24 and Johnson's Epistemology." *Modern Philology* 64 (1966):10–21.

Richards, I[vor] A[rmstrong]. *Practical Criticism: A Study of Literary Judgment.* 1929. New York: Harvest-Harcourt, n.d.

Richman, Jordan. "Johnson as a Swiftian Satirist." *University of Dayton Review* 7.2 (1970–71):21–28.

————. "Subjectivity in the Art of Eighteenth-Century Biography: Johnson's Portrait of Swift." *Enlightenment Essays* 2 (1971):91–102.

Rogers, Pat. "Johnson's *Lives of the Poets* and the Biographic Dictionaries." *Review of English Studies* 31 (1980):149–71.

Rothstein, Eric. *Systems of Order and Inquiry in Later Eighteenth-Century Fiction.* Berkeley: U of California P, 1975.

Ruml, Treadwell II. "The Younger Johnson's Texts of Pope." *Review of English Studies* n.s. 36 (1985):180–98.

178

Bibliography

Sachs, Arieh. *Passionate Intelligence: Imagination and Reason in the Work of Samuel Johnson*. Baltimore: Johns Hopkins UP, 1967.

Schwartz, Richard B. *Boswell's Johnson: A Preface to the Life*. Madison: U of Wisconsin P, 1978.

———. "Dr. Johnson and the Satiric Reaction to Science." *Studies in Burke and His Time* 11 (1969):1336–47.

———. *Samuel Johnson and the New Science*. Madison: U of Wisconsin P, 1971.

———. *Samuel Johnson and the Problem of Evil*. Madison: U of Wisconsin P, 1975.

Sextus Empiricus. *Outlines of Pyrrhonism*. Trans. R. G. Bury. Loeb Classical Library. Cambridge: Harvard UP, 1933.

Shackleton, Robert. "Johnson and the Enlightenment." *Johnson, Boswell, and Their Circle: Essays Presented to Lawrence Fitzroy Powell in Honour of His Eighty-Fourth Birthday*. Oxford: Clarendon, 1965. 76–92.

Shapiro, Barbara J. *Probability and Certainty in Seventeenth-Century England: A Study of the Relationships between Natural Science, Religion, History, Law, and Literature*. Princeton: Princeton UP, 1983.

Shapiro, David. *Neurotic Styles*. Austen Riggs Center Monograph Series 5. New York: Basic, 1965.

Sherbo, Arthur. "Johnson's *Shakespeare* and the Dramatic Criticism in the *Lives of the English Poets*." *Shakespeare: Aspects of Influence*. Ed. G[wynne] B[lakemore] Evans. Harvard English Studies 7. Cambridge: Harvard UP, 1976. 55–67.

Siebenschuh, William R. "On the Locus of Faith in Johnson's Sermons." *Studies in Burke and His Time* 17 (1976):103–17.

Siebert, Donald T[ate], Jr. "Johnson and Hume on Miracles." *Journal of the History of Ideas* 36 (1975):543–47.

———. "Samuel Johnson and the Style of Satire." Diss. U of Virginia, 1972.

Sigworth, Oliver F. "Johnson's *Lycidas:* The End of Renaissance Criticism." *Eighteenth-Century Studies* 1 (1967):159–68.

———. "Reply to Victor J. Milne." *Eighteenth-Century Studies* 2 (1969): 301–2.

Smallwood, P. J. "Johnson's *Life of Pope* and Pope's Preface to the *Iliad.*" *Notes and Queries* 27 (1980):50.

————. "Samuel Johnson and Dryden's 'Contempt' for Otway." *Notes and Queries* 27 (1980):49–50.

Stanlis, Peter J. "Comment on 'Samuel Johnson and "Natural Law."'" *Journal of British Studies* 2.2 (1963):76–83.

Starobinski, Jean. "Criticism and Authority." *Daedalus* 106.4 (1977):1–16. [Trans. A. Cancogni and R. Sieburth.]

Stauffer, Donald. *The Art of Biography in Eighteenth Century England.* 2 vols. 1941; New York: Russell & Russell, 1970.

Stephen, Leslie. *History of English Thought in the Eighteenth Century.* 3rd ed. 2 vols. 1902. New York: Harbinger-Harcourt, 1962.

Sternbach, Robert. "Pascal and Dr. Johnson on Immortality." *Journal of the History of Ideas* 39 (1978):483–89.

Strachey, Lytton. *Books and Characters, French and English.* New York: Harcourt, 1922.

Sullivan, Victoria D[iane]. "The Biographies of Samuel Johnson: A Study of the Relationship of the Biographer to His Subject." Diss. Columbia U, 1969.

Sun, Phillip S. Y. "Swift's Eighteenth-Century Biographies." Diss. Yale U, 1963.

Swearingen, James E. "Johnson's 'Life of Gray.'" *Texas Studies in Literature and Language* 14 (1972):283–302.

Swift, Deane. *An Essay upon the Life, Writings, and Character, of Dr. Jonathan Swift.* London: 1755.

Swift, Jonathan. *The Correspondence of Jonathan Swift.* Ed. Harold Williams. 5 vols. Oxford: Clarendon, 1963–65.

————. *The Works of the Rev. Jonathan Swift, D.D.* Ed. John Nichols. 19 vols. London: 1801.

Tarbet, David W. "Lockean 'Intuition' and Johnson's Characterization of Aesthetic Response." *Eighteenth-Century Studies* 5 (1971):58–79.

Tavor, Eve. *Scepticism, Society, and the Eighteenth-Century Novel.* New York: St. Martin's, 1987.

Teerink, Herman. *A Bibliography of the Writings of Jonathan Swift.* Ed.

180

Bibliography

Arthur H. Scouten. 2nd ed. Philadelphia: U of Pennsylvania P, 1963.

Tillinghast, Anthony J. "The Moral and Philosophical Basis of Johnson's and Boswell's Idea of Biography." Wahba 115–31.

Tracy, Clarence. *The Artificial Bastard: A Biography of Richard Savage.* Cambridge: Harvard UP, 1953.

———. "Boswell: The Cautious Empiricist." *The Triumph of Culture: Eighteenth-Century Perspectives.* Ed. Paul Fritz and David Williams. Publications of the McMaster University Association for Eighteenth-Century Studies 2. Toronto: Hakkert, 1972. 225–43.

———. *Life of Savage.* Oxford: Clarendon, 1971.

Treglown, Jeremy. "Scepticism and Parody in the Restoration." *Modern Language Review* 75 (1980):18–47.

Trowbridge, Hoyt. "The Language of Reasoned Rhetoric in *The Rambler.*" Korshin and Allen 200–16.

———. "Scattered Atoms of Probability." *Eighteenth-Century Studies* 5 (1971):1–38.

———. "White of Selborne: The Ethos of Probabilism." *From Dryden to Jane Austen: Essays on English Critics and Writers, 1660–1818.* By H. Trowbridge. Albuquerque: U of New Mexico P, 1977. 249–72.

Uhlman, Thompson Potter. "The Reputation of Samuel Johnson's *The Lives of the Poets,* in England and America." Diss. U of Southern California, 1968.

Uphaus, Robert W. "The 'Equipoise' of Johnson's *Life of Savage.*" *Studies in Burke and His Time* 17 (1976):43–54.

———. *The Impossible Observer: Reason and the Reader in Eighteenth-Century Prose.* Lexington: UP of Kentucky, 1979.

Vance, John A., ed. *Boswell's "Life of Johnson": New Questions, New Answers.* Athens: U of Georgia P, 1985.

Van Leeuwen, Henry G. *The Problem of Certainty in English Thought, 1630–1690.* International Archives of the History of Ideas 3. 2nd ed. The Hague: Martinus Nijhoff, 1970.

Vesterman, William. "Johnson and *The Life of Savage.*" *ELH* 36 (1969): 659–78.

———. *The Stylistic Life of Samuel Johnson.* New Brunswick: Rutgers UP, 1977.

181

Bibliography

Voitle, Robert. *Samuel Johnson the Moralist.* Cambridge: Harvard UP, 1961.

Wahba, Magdi, ed. *Johnsonian Studies.* Cairo: S.O.P.-Press, 1962.

Waldman, Theodore. "Origins of the Legal Doctrine of Reasonable Doubt." *Journal of the History of Ideas* 20 (1959):299–316.

Walker, Robert G. "Johnson in the 'Age of Evidences.'" *Huntington Library Quarterly* 44 (1980):27–41.

———. "Johnson, Tillotson, and Comparative Credibility." *Notes and Queries* 24 (1977):254–55.

Warncke, Wayne. "Samuel Johnson on Swift: The *Life of Swift* and Johnson's Predecessors in Swiftian Biography." *Journal of British Studies* 7 (1968):56–64.

Watkins, Walter B[arker] C[ritz]. *Perilous Balance: The Tragic Genius of Swift, Johnson, & Sterne.* 1939. Cambridge: Walker–de Berry, 1960.

Weinbrot, Howard D. "John Clarke's *Essay on Study* and Samuel Johnson on *Paradise Lost*." *Modern Philology* 72 (1974):404–7.

Weinsheimer, Joel. *Imitation.* London: Routledge, 1984.

Wendorf, Richard. "The Making of Johnson's 'Life of Collins.'" *Papers of the Bibliographical Society of America* 74 (1980):95–115.

Wharton, T. F. *Samuel Johnson and the Theme of Hope.* New York: St. Martin's, 1984.

Wiley, Margaret L. *The Subtle Knot: Creative Scepticism in Seventeenth-Century England.* London: Allen, 1952.

Williams, Harold. "Swift's Early Biographers." *Pope and His Contemporaries: Essays Presented to George Sherburn.* Ed. James L. Clifford and Louis A. Landa. 1949. New York: Octagon-Farrar, 1978. 114–28.

Wimsatt, W[illiam] K., Jr. *Philosophic Words: A Study of Style and Meaning in the "Rambler" and "Dictionary" of Samuel Johnson.* 1948. n.p.: Archon, 1968.

———. *The Prose Style of Samuel Johnson.* Yale Studies in English 94. 1941. Hamden: Archon-Shoe String, 1972.

Wright, John W. "Samuel Johnson and Traditional Methodology." *PMLA* 86 (1971):40–50.

Index

Index

Index